DAG
HAMMARSKJÖLD

By Charlie May Simon

DAG
HAMMARSKJÖLD
BY
CHARLIE MAY SIMON

E. P. DUTTON & CO., INC.
NEW YORK

The poems and journal extracts from *Markings* by Dag Hammarskjöld, translated by Leif Sjoberg and W. H. Auden, are used with the permission of Alfred A. Knopf, Inc. Copyright © 1964 by Alfred A. Knopf, Inc. and Faber and Faber Ltd.

The poem on page 85 is reprinted by permission of Harvard University Press from *Tu Fu: China's Greatest Poet* by William Hung. Copyright 1952 by the President and Fellows of Harvard College.

The photographs facing pages 48, 49, 80, and 81 are used through the courtesy of the Swedish Information Agency and Mr. Bo Hammarskjöld. The photographs facing pages 112, 113, 144, and 145 are used through the courtesy of the United Nations.

To the memory of my parents
Charles and Mary Hogue

CONTENTS

DAG
HAMMARSKJÖLD

ONE

1905–1913

A well-loved child, it is said in Sweden, is given many names. Dag Hjalmar Agne Carl Hammarskjöld, born July 9, 1905, would grow up to be well-loved all over the world, but he had to wait four months for his many names. There was deep anxiety in Sweden at the time of his birth, with the threat of war hanging over the country.

Norway, after a union of almost a hundred years, was demanding complete independence. Hjalmar Hammarskjöld, the child's father, then Minister of Education in the Swedish cabinet, was sent as one of four delegates to negotiate with the Norwegians. They met at Karlstadt, halfway between the capitals of the two countries, where the discussions dragged on and on. It was late autumn before an agreement could be reached to dissolve the union. Hjalmar Hammarskjöld had felt that, united, the two countries could put up a stronger defense against possible aggression, and he called it appeasement to give in to Norway's demands. But, since it was also important to keep Sweden's long record of peace, he agreed in the end with his fellow negotiators and signed the treaty of separation and perpetual friendship.

The Swedish king then publicly renounced his claim to Norway's crown and the Norwegians chose a king of their own. And Sweden's prime minister with all his cabinet turned in their resignations. It was not until November that Hjalmar Hammarskjöld was free to return home for the christening of his fourth son.

The family was living then in a stately mansion called the Villa Liljehoben in the town of Jönköping on the southern shores of Lake Vätter. Friends came to the christening from as far away as Stockholm. They drank a toast to the child Dag, whose name meant the "light of day." And they drank a toast to peace. In a prominent place among the many christening presents there was a silver cup with the inscription "For the one too long without a name," given by the father's fellow negotiators.

After his resignation from the cabinet, Hjalmar Hammarskjöld was appointed Sweden's ambassador to Denmark. Shortly after the christening of his youngest son, he left Jönköping with his family to take up residence at the Swedish Embassy in Copenhagen. Two years later he was called back to Sweden and made lord lieutenant of Uppland Province.

The move was a welcome one for Hjalmar Hammarskjöld. It was something of a homecoming to him, for he had gone to Uppsala from his native province Småland as a schoolboy of ten, and had stayed on for twenty years—through all his student days and as a teacher at the University.

In Denmark, he had been concerned about the education of his sons. Bo and Åke were sixteen and fourteen and were already making plans for college. Sten, the third son, was seven and just starting to school, and soon enough the baby Dag would be ready for kindergarten. Sweden's oldest and finest university was at Uppsala. Here the boys could live at home with the family during their student years; they would not have to leave as he had done. Nor would they have the hardship and struggle to make ends meet that had been his. Though the Hammarskjölds were an old, aristocratic family, they had long ago lost their fortune. Hjalmar Hammarskjöld had had the care of his mother and younger brothers, as well as his own expenses, to meet. It was only through his brilliant record and scholarships that he had been able to complete his education.

Now, as lord lieutenant, he and his family lived in the red brick castle that had been standing for more than four hundred years on a high hill overlooking the town of Uppsala. It was a place where the kings of Sweden had once resided, but in recent years it had been turned into living quarters and administrative offices for the governors of the province.

The child Dag was to know no earlier home than the old castle on the hill. His first sure steps, beyond the faltering ones of a baby, were on its worn stone floors, and his first impressions of the outside world were from the deeply recessed windows where he could look out over the rooftops, beyond the spires and towers of the Cathedral, to the far horizon where earth and sky seem to meet.

On a pedestal facing the window of his room, there was a bronze bust of Gustavus I of the Vasa dynasty. In winter, the snow streaked his beard and gave him a jaunty white cap such as the students of Uppsala wore on festive occasions; and often in summer a bird, pausing in its flight, perched on his laurel-crowned head. But the old king, as stern and dignified as Dag's father, stared on at this castle he had commanded to be built so many years ago.

Twice the castle had been damaged by fire and never fully restored. Many of the rooms were now deserted and bare, but once this had been as magnificent as any castle in Europe. The walls had been hung with paintings and tapestries, and the rooms decorated with ornaments of ivory, amber, and gold. At the upper end of the great south hall, where Sweden's kings sometimes held court, there had been a silver throne with cushions and canopy of crimson velvet.

Sometimes, on a stormy night when the ceiling timbers squeaked and groaned and the ancient trees rubbed their branches one against the other, sounds like footsteps might be heard, as of ghosts returning to once familiar places. There had been dancing and flirting and secret plotting in these rooms long ago, and feasts that lasted as long as seven days, with whole oxen roasting on spits and fountains flowing with wine. And down in the dungeons men were chained in darkness for real or imagined wrongs. With his own hands, Sweden's mad King Eric had killed one, a nobleman whom he feared.

Three centuries ago, a lonely little girl, wandering through these rooms dressed as a boy, had been called a prince. She was Christina, the only child of Gustavus Adolphus, the grandson of Gustavus Vasa. Her mother, who had prayed long for a son, turned her face to the wall in bitterness at her daughter's birth and would have nothing to do with her. When the child was six, her father was killed in battle, leaving her heir to the throne. Christina had herself crowned king—not queen—of Sweden when she came of age, and she reigned for ten years. Then one day, in the great south hall of this castle, she stood facing her senate. She solemnly removed the crown from her head, threw off her royal purple robe, and, clad only in a simple white gown, renounced forever for herself and her heirs the throne of Sweden.

The silver throne has long been gone from the room, and the ornaments of ivory, amber, and gold are scattered in museums. And the dungeons have become nothing more than caves for the curious to explore. With the coming of the Hammarskjölds, the old walls echoed with the sounds of boys at play. It was a glorious place for a child to grow up in.

A child was fortunate to be born in the Hammarskjöld family with its heritage of intellect and leadership. But he had a demanding life ahead of him, one filled with responsibilities. Since 1610, when the first Hammar-

skjöld, a cavalry officer, was knighted and given his
name, meaning "hammer and shield," there had been
soldiers and statesmen in the family who devoted their
lives to the service of their country and king. Hjalmar
Hammarskjöld followed in this tradition and his sons
knew at an early age that they would do the same.

The mother, Agnes, was warm and outgoing, as affectionate and gentle as the father was stern. Before the
birth of her youngest child, she had prayed for a
daughter, one who would be a companion to her while
the three older children prepared themselves to follow in
the footsteps of the father. She was forty then and knew
this child would be her last. Unlike the mother of Christina, she felt no bitterness when she learned she had
borne another son. She lavished more love on him than if
he had been the daughter she had wanted. She delighted
in his fair complexion and eyes as blue as the summer
skies. She dressed him in dainty clothes trimmed in
ruffles and lace, and let his hair grow to his shoulders in
golden ringlets, as many a romantic mother of her time
did.

Sten, five years older, was one day to remember the
time when he quit his play to follow the baby in his
pram as the nursemaid, Erna, wheeled him to the park.
"When I saw how sweet he was, lying there smiling, I
forgot what I had been intending to do," he wrote in
later years. "I loved the little fellow. When Erna put the
pram beside the rose trellis and walked a short distance
away, I climbed up on one of the wheels to kiss him, but
the pram tipped over. I rushed away afraid."

The child had a happy disposition, and little hurts of babyhood were quickly forgotten. He was tenderly sheltered and protected, with the older brothers petting him as much as his parents did. Sometimes they took time to play with him, but he was as content to play alone. In the garden close to the castle wall, his legs wet with early morning dew, he dragged his toy cart with its wooden horse on rollers, or, with a toy rake, he tried to heap the fallen leaves as the gardeners were doing. The park, with its ancient trees, was a wonderful primeval forest to him. Giant mushrooms like gnomes sprang up overnight on the forest floor. Every day brought some new wonder for him to explore: a raindrop trickling down the windowpane, the whispering of lilacs beneath his bedroom window, the linden trees in bloom, perfuming the air with their heavy fragrance.

He saw that in midwinter, when the snow covered the ground and the gnarled old trees in the castle park were stiff and bare, the sun rose late, long after he had had his breakfast, only to set again soon after in a long blue twilight. Shadowy beings seemed to move restlessly throughout the castle, in all the corners and alcoves and over the great stone stairs. Then in midsummer, when the earth had come back to life with green leaves and grass and the song of birds, he saw the light of one day merge with the light of the next, and the darkness was brief. The sun still shone through the open window at bedtime when the family gathered for evening prayers and song and the mother read a chapter from the Bible.

Every Sunday Dag went with his mother to the

Cathedral. The building was old, far older than the castle. For almost eight hundred years people had come here to worship, and before that there was an ancient grove on this site, sacred to the old gods, Odin, Freyr, and Thor. Dag sat in the pew beside his mother, quiet and meditative. This place had become as familiar as home to him, yet its splendor still gave him delight. His eyes followed the fluted columns that supported the high vaulted ceiling. Like tall trees, they reached up toward the heavens. The sparkling chandeliers were like clusters of stars shining down on the gilded statues of saints and the bowed heads of the worshipers. Here the kings of Sweden had been crowned long ago. Many of them were buried in the chapels along the sides. The marble figure of old Gustavus I of Vasalay in royal robes above his tomb, between two of his wives; a third wife was buried in a chapel nearby. Behind the altar there was a silver casket containing the bones of Eric, the patron saint of the Cathedral.

"Almighty God, most fervently do we pray that the example of Thy saints may stir our deep longing for a holy life," the minister read from the Book of Prayer.

When the music rolled forth from the organ in the loft, Dag joined in the singing even before he could read the words in the hymnal:

> Nought is given 'neath the sun.
> Nought is had that is not won.

It was said of the Hammarskjölds that they were a hard-working family. "The father had a strong character," a friend of Dag's wrote in later years. "He wanted his sons to realize the necessity of work, and his sons accepted the challenge."

Hjalmar Hammarskjöld was the opposite of his wife in temperament. He was formal and austere. To see him walking along the streets of Uppsala or Stockholm, wearing a frock coat and a high silk hat and swinging a gold-headed cane, one knew at a glance that he was a man of authority.

Often Dag looked up from his play and listened, with a child's limited understanding, while the father discussed public affairs with the older brothers or gave them advice in their studies. Sometimes he talked about Väderum, the old family estate in Småland where he had lived as a child. It was his great regret that it had had to be sold, after so many generations in the family, because of the heavy expense in keeping it up. Life had been paternalistic there. The children of peasants and farm workers had been his playmates before he left for school, and they had told him tales, which they seriously believed, of trolls and pixies and little tomtar elves that lived in the lofts of houses and took an interest in the family affairs.

Hjalmar Hammarskjöld's sons grew up in an atmosphere of old traditions, where the customs of a bygone day were still followed. Holidays and festivals were kept as his people had always kept them. At Easter the boys wrote verses on their eggs before they were dyed, just as he had done; Dag's small hand was guided to form the letters of his verse before he had learned to write. On Midsummer Eve the family went for a ride in an open carriage, with the coachman sitting in front, flicking his whip at the horse's back. They drove past neat red farmhouses and plowed fields where summer flowers bloomed. A daughter on this day would have danced, with the other young girls of town, around a gaily beribboned Maypole. And on St. Lucia's Day, twelve days before Christmas, she would have come at dawn into the family bedrooms, bearing a tray with coffee and sweet rolls. She would have been dressed in a long, white robe, and on her head would have been a crown of greenery set with lighted candles, a tribute to the sun's return, bringing warmth, fertility, and life.

Christmas was the festival most loved in all the year. Dag and his brother Sten were allowed to go with the father down to the market place across the river Fyris, to select the Christmas tree. Green garlands of fir were draped over doorways of shops and from one lamppost to another. In every lighted window there were Christmas toys—straw-plaited billy goats and tomtar, made of knitting yarn, with long white beards, red suits, and stocking caps trimmed in white. The snow-covered sidewalks were lined with freshly cut fir trees, as if a forest had sprung up overnight. The vendors shivered and stamped their feet to keep warm, but everyone was in a good humor and called cheerful greetings to each other.

On Christmas Eve, the father began the evening meal by cutting, with great ceremony, into an enormous round cheese, a gift the Dairy Association made every year to their chairman. The long dining table was set in the old-fashioned way, as at Småland, with dishes of

ham and *lutfish*, and all the rich Christmas foods. When
they had finished eating, they gathered with the family servants around the great tree, bright now with
flickering candles and colored ornaments. Before the gifts
were distributed, Agnes Hammarskjöld read from the
Lutheran prayer book, and all joined her in singing
Christmas hymns. The Christmas hymns were joyous
ones—of Mary and the Child Jesus, of shepherds watching their flocks by night, and angels proclaiming peace
on earth to men of good will. But never would an old
year pass that Dag Hammarskjöld would not remember
the words of the song they sang on New Year's Eve,
"Soon comes the night."

Dag would watch his mother's face in the soft glow of
the lamp as she read and sang. It was still youthful, with
delicate, regular features. Her hair was dark, and worn
high on her head in the fashion of the time. When she
looked up from her page, her dark eyes shone with
affection for them all. Out beyond the darkened windows, the familiar daytime scenes had disappeared and
an immense strange world of mysterious shadows and
sounds had taken their place. But here in this room,
where no harm could reach him, the boy felt sheltered
and protected. The mother, romantic and sentimental,
was quick to show her love, but the father's love lay
hidden beneath an air of stern dignity.

Dag inherited the traits of both his parents. Like his
father he was fair, with light hair and blue eyes, and he
had his father's quick mind and tireless energy. There
was a reserve about him even as a small child that kept

him from making close friends; yet beneath that reserve, he had the warm and sensitive spirit of his mother.

Under the mother's guidance he developed spiritually, but it was the father who saw to the development of the boy's mind. When he reached school age, his hair was cut short and he was dressed in the clothes of a school-boy. First he was enrolled in a private kindergarten, and later at the public primary school.

The first of Dag's childhood companions was Jon Olaf Söderblom, son of his parents' closest friends. Nathan Söderblom, later to become Archbishop, was then a pro-fessor of theology at the University. The boys were about the same age and were classmates from the time they started to kindergarten together. Both were robust and active. They played games together on the school grounds or ran races in and out among the great trees of the castle park. In winter they learned to skate on the frozen river Fyris and slid on the snow-packed paths leading down the hill. In summer they swam in the blue waters of Eklon, the northern tip of Lake Mälaren.

Schoolwork was easy for him from the beginning. He began to read from primers, and he wrote exercises in copybooks, taking care not to leave a blot on the page. He learned to use the umlaut over the *a* and *o* to indicate pronunciation. He could write Hammarskjöld, Söder-blom, Åke, Småland.

In his father's library there was a wide choice of books for a boy just learning the pleasure of reading. There were books of all sizes, some very old with leather or parchment bindings, and some with illustrations which had fascinated him when the printed lines were still an unsolved mystery to him.

Among Dag's earliest favorites were the books of Carl Linnaeus, the great eighteenth-century botanist, who had taught at Uppsala and whose body lay buried beneath the stone floors of the Cathedral. Linnaeus had written poetically about the Swedish countryside, yet in a style simple enough for a child to understand. He could make the reader see meadows glow with yellow butter-cups, hear the magpies playing a creaking bass in the tall dry trees, or catch the scent of juniper in the warm air. His words opened Dag's eyes to the wonders of simple things about him, things so ordinary that others might scarcely notice them: the orange shimmer in the setting winter sun; an alder tree by the water's edge, pale olive against pewter, its bare branches moved by the waves. In the shadow of the castle the first frost appeared and there the summer flowers closed long before nightfall.

There was a garden not far from the castle planted in memory of Carl Linnaeus with the flowers and shrubs of Sweden in all their varieties and tagged with the names and classifications the botanist had given them. There Dag learned to know the common primrose and the marsh marigold by their Latin names, and he saw the rare fritillary, so like a snake's head, come into bloom.

He found a friend, Bo Tigerschiöld, who shared his enthusiasm in collecting plants and insects. The gardens and park around the castle were a hunting ground full of hidden treasures. They dug under the leaf mold in search of a purple orchis, and they tried to find the checkered daffodil. With butterfly nets they hunted moths and butterflies. Once they found a rare *Limentitis Populi* on a pile of dung.

"What is an idyll?" Bo asked one day.

Dag, then eight years old, took his friend's notebook and wrote in it, "An idyll is a lamb with a blue ribbon on it."

In that year, the Indian poet Rabindranath Tagore called at the castle after winning the Nobel Prize. His poems, read aloud, brought to the listeners a sense of the wonder and mysticism of the East. As a member of the Swedish Royal Academy, Hjalmar Hammarskjöld was one of the judges for the Nobel Prize in literature and so was personally acquainted with many of the modern authors. They, as well as scientists and men prominent in government affairs, were often entertained at the castle. On occasion the king and queen came there as guests also.

Dag listened meditatively to the grown-up talk around him and his mind tried to grasp something he could understand and remember. He heard his father and Nathan Söderblom, who shared an interest in the ancient classics, discuss Greek drama and philosophy and the religions of the East. Sometimes, in family conversations, stories were told of Swedish history or of some ancestor long dead. Dag's imagination was busy with people and events of the past. On both sides of the family, there had been poets: Lorenzo Hammarskjöld, a great-uncle of his father, and Carl Jonas Love Almqvist, his mother's great-uncle. Both men had a touch of genius

and were an important influence on Swedish literature.
And there were the ancestors, father and son, who fought
with Charles XII, and that first Hammarskjöld who had
served Charles IX. The blood of all flowed through the
boy's veins. He thought of them and he was filled with
indefinite dreams and longings. What would his own life
be like? he wondered. The future was like a dense curtain, too heavy for him to lift.

There was a deep family affection between him and
his brothers, but the difference in their ages was too great
for the intimacy of brothers who were closer in years.
Sten was an adolescent while Dag was still a child, and
Bo and Åke were young men reaching the end of their
student years.

The friendships he formed at this time were to be
lasting ones. His classmates found him fun to be with. He
was good at sports, and he had a quick mind and ready
wit. In games of competition each side wanted him for a
leader. But from the beginning there was something that
kept him from feeling part of a group. He had loyal
friends, but no close ones.

"He was a good comrade who remained loyal to his
friends all his life," Jon Olaf wrote of him later. "As a
boy he was a completely natural and amusing play-
mate. But not one we could get intimate with."

Dag made the highest grades in the class without the
long hours of study and effort the others had to put in.
And he was the son of the lord lieutenant of the province,
living in a castle away from the other houses of town.
These things alone were enough to set a boy apart from

his companions. But with young Dag, there was something more. As with every sensitive child, there was an inner self, a self reserved for ideals and dreams and glimpses of beauty which he could not bring himself to share. And with it, there was a loneliness that would never leave him.

T W O

1914–1924

"Soon comes the night." The sweet voice of Agnes Hammarskjöld sang with her family as the midnight bells rang out the old year and rang in the new.

The year 1914 brought a sense of foreboding. There was a strange kind of restlessness over all of Europe then. The major powers had been at peace for almost half a century, but it was a peace that still clung to old hates and rivalries. Now alliances were formed and nations were arming heavily. Germany, allied with Austria, was building a powerful navy, and England, with France and Russia on her side, matched it two to one. Germany had military conscription, and France began a three-year training program for her men.

Sweden refused to join either side in an alliance, but the people were divided over whether or not to arm as the countries surrounding them were do-

27

ing. The two leading parties carried on angry debates in Parliament. The Conservatives believed that only by a strong military defense could the country remain neutral, and the Liberals thought that building up their armed forces could easily lead to war. On a raw cold day in February, thirty thousand peasants gathered at Stockholm from all parts of the country. They staged a march on the Royal Palace and, going over the head of Parliament, appealed directly to the king for a strong defense. The king, without consulting his government, replied, agreeing with the peasants. This caused an outcry among the Liberals, for the king had gone beyond his rights in a constitutional monarchy. As a result, the prime minister and all his cabinet resigned.

Hjalmar Hammarskjöld had just returned from Russia where he had been sent on a mission of negotiation the month before. Now, at the king's request, he accepted the post of prime minister and formed a new cabinet, though he was not a member of any political party. Four months after he took office, news came over the telegraph wires of the world that the heir to the Austrian throne and his wife had been assassinated by a young Serb, to avenge the seizure of his country.

Events followed, one after the other, as if they had been well rehearsed. Austria declared war on Serbia; Germany declared war on Russia and France and, on August 3, sent troops marching into Belgium; Britain came in on the side of France, with Japan and Italy following soon after; and Turkey entered the war on Germany's side. By November, the war had spread over

most of Europe and into Africa and Asia. The three
Scandinavian countries remained neutral, but they signed
an agreement to act jointly in case any one of them was
attacked.

Dag Hammarskjöld, as son of the prime minister, was
more aware of what was happening than other boys his
age. This was a war like no other war before it. For the
first time, attacks were made from the air and from
under the sea, and the victims were not limited to men in
combat. Wherever a bomb struck, it brought death and
destruction to everybody and everything around it.
Old people and babies, the sick and the helpless alike,
were killed.

Less and less respect was shown for the rights of
neutrals under international law. Both the Germans and
the Allies wanted to force Sweden into their trade war,
but Hjalmar Hammarskjöld refused to take any action
that would be considered warlike by either side. His
main concern was to keep his country neutral, and
because of this he became a target of criticism on all
sides. The old conflict between Sweden's leading political
parties flared up again, this time over foreign policy,
and both turned on the prime minister. He kept his trade
agreements with England and France and he was accused
of favoring the Allies; and he was called a tool of Germany when he kept his trade agreements with that
country.

"My policy is Swedish and nothing but Swedish," he
declared.

The war dragged on longer than anyone had believed

possible, and in time Sweden's own resources were low. Foreign trade was curtailed, and the government had to confiscate important goods and establish rationing and fixed prices. Food, especially, was extremely scarce, and the people began calling their prime minister "Hunger-skjöld."

In the spring of 1917, Hjalmar Hammarskjöld bowed to his political enemies and turned in his resignation, along with the members of his cabinet. The United States had come into the war against Germany in February; and in March, the Russian Empire had collapsed, with the Bolshevists preparing to take over. In Sweden, there was another crisis in the government.

The father's unpopularity affected Dag perhaps more than it did the older brothers. Some of his classmates, taking on the prejudices of their elders without fully understanding them, taunted him and made him feel unwanted in their games. Often now he could only stand aside and watch them have fun. He was learning early the price a man must pay who is impartial in his judgments and refuses to be swayed from his own convictions.

The boy was growing in wisdom and in body, and his thoughts were no longer only those of a child. In the gray twilight, when the air was mild and overflowing with the fragrance of honeysuckle, a feeling came over him of inexpressible joy touched with sadness. He felt, in his own growth, a kinship with all growing things, with the lark singing deliriously, its wings quivering, with the wasp hunting among the white peonies, with the swallows like black shooting stars, uttering their shrill cries.

A teeming world of life murmured and buzzed all about him, in the air and on the forest floor, each life acting out its drama of ecstasy and tragedy: a cotillion of butterflies like dancing girls and a spider coming out of her nook to ensnare one in her web; a young hare nibbling tender shoots of a shrub and a goshawk circling to swoop; a lizard sunning itself and an adder coiled in the wild strawberry patch. Little school children in Uppsala played soldier with paper caps and wooden swords, and in France men were still fighting and dying.

Hjalmar Hammarskjöld took up his duties again as governor of the province with the same concern he had shown in international affairs. He went about the countryside and talked with the peasants about their problems, and he made plans for improvements in roads, schools, and agriculture for Uppland.

He was still criticized in the newspapers and magazines of Stockholm. Dag read that his father had been autocratic, had made decisions without consulting other officials of the government, stubbornly believing that only he was right. But Dag did not look upon him that way, nor did his older brothers. Whatever his enemies said of Hjalmar Hammarskjöld, none doubted his integrity and his strong sense of justice. His loyalty to his country remained as steadfast as ever, though he no longer took part in national or international affairs.

Long after, in looking back upon this period, Dag would say in defense of his father, "A mature man is his own judge. The advice of others may be welcome and valuable, but it does not free him from responsibility. Therefore he may be very lonely. Therefore too, he, with open eyes, may run the risk of being accused of stubborn self-sufficiency. As the war went on, this was the fate of Hjalmar Hammarskjöld."

The war lasted until 1918. After the bloodshed and destruction of four and a half years, there was a demand among the people of the world for some means of preventing future wars. With planes and submarines and faster ways of communication, the destinies of all nations were linked together. When a minor conflict such as the one between Austria and Serbia could flare into a war that spread over the whole world, there would be no place, however remote, that could escape the disasters of another one.

The International Court at The Hague was dedicated to the cause of peace through negotiations and international law. Hjalmar Hammarskjöld had been Sweden's leading delegate there during its early years. Now it was made stronger, and another organization, the League of Nations, was formed, with the noble purpose of keeping the peace through justice instead of force. No member nation was to declare war before an attempt was made to bring about a peaceful solution. And there must be no more secret treaties which could pledge a country to fight without the knowledge of its nationals.

Dag was fourteen when the League of Nations held its first meeting in Geneva, old enough to take an interest in it and form his own opinions. He was now included in the family discussions, and the talk often turned to this new hope for world peace. Sweden was one of the original members, and Åke was sent abroad by the government, from time to time, on some mission of conciliation. Like his father before him, he was also a delegate to The Hague Court. The following year, when he was twenty-nine, he was made its Secretary-General.

A new industrial growth followed the war; and with it came an idealism and a renewed belief in justice and peace, and concern for one's fellow man. Dag Hammar-skjöld was to look back on this period as "that strange brief idyll that burgeoned all over Europe between two crises and two wars." In Uppsala it had a quality all its own, he said.

Nathan Söderblom became Archbishop of Uppsala in the same year that Hjalmar Hammarskjöld was made prime minister, and through his efforts to unite the churches of the world, Uppsala was becoming an inter-national center. He believed that the depth of a man's spiritual beliefs were more important than the way he worshiped, and he wanted to see the spirit of religion brought into all of man's relationships, in his social, economic, and industrial life.

It was natural that Dag Hammarskjöld, coming into adolescence in this atmosphere, should choose for his heroes spiritual men—the mystics and saints. The first to influence him was Söderblom whom he had admired since childhood. Another and even greater influence on his life was Albert Schweitzer. At the invitation of Arch-bishop Söderblom, Schweitzer came to Uppsala in the spring of 1920 to give a series of lectures. He came there sick, tired, and depressed. For four years he had been confined as a prisoner of war in France, for at that time Alsace, his native home, had been a part of Germany. He had been forced to leave his jungle hospital in Africa, and, to keep it going during his absence, he had gone heavily into debt. The Archbishop, guessing his plight, arranged lectures and organ recitals for him in other parts of Sweden also.

He became a familiar figure in Uppsala, with his shock of unruly hair and his black woolen suit with black bow tie. He played the old organ of the Cathedral as it had never been played before. And his lectures at the University gave his listeners new ideas to meditate upon. His last lecture at the University was on "Reverence for Life," a maxim which Dag Hammarskjöld would make his own: "If I am a thinking being, I must regard other life than my own with equal reverence. For I shall know that it longs for fulness and development as deeply as I do myself."

Schweitzer was unaware of the lord lieutenant's youngest son, fifteen at that time, growing tall and gangly, and filled with the idealism of youth. The two were destined never to meet, but they would become friends through an exchange of letters and a sharing of thoughts and beliefs.

At the age of seventeen, Dag Hammarskjöld took his entrance examinations to the University. His grades were the highest, but his father, stern and exacting, had set a high goal for his sons. His only remark was, "Åke did better." Neither Åke nor Dag, however, did as well as the father. He had received his Bachelor of Arts degree when he was eighteen. Dag received his at nineteen.

During his undergraduate years, Dag majored in languages and literature. There was a time when, inspired by Nathan Söderblom, he thought of taking up theology, but by the time he was ready for graduate work, he knew that he would follow his father and older brothers in a career as public servant. For the next three years he studied political economy.

The students of Uppsala were caught up in the wave of idealism that followed the war. The works of Karl Marx and Freud were popular among them, and they read Spengler's *Decline of the West*. They could be seen walking along the banks of the Fyris or gathered together in coffee shops in serious discussions about their country's future. Once the lot of Sweden's peasants and workers had been so unbearable that they were forced to migrate in order to feed and clothe their families. Since 1850, over a million, one-seventh of the country's total population, had gone to America. Many were of the nation's finest in health, strength, and intelligence, and wherever they went, they gave their strength to their new country and added to its greatness. But Sweden needed such men and women at home and something must be done to keep them. Some of the students looked to Russia and the new Communism for the answer. Others argued that social reforms could be brought about without a totalitarian regime and the loss of freedom that goes with it.

Instead of fraternities at the University there were clubs or nations where students were grouped according to their home town provinces. Hjalmar Hammarskjöld had belonged to the Småland Nation, but his four sons were Uppland members. But Dag, like his older brothers, continued to live with his parents at the castle instead of with the students in town. Many a time a group of students, after a long and unsolved discussion, would walk up the hill and call for Dag, to get his point of view. And Dag and the young students, many of whom were later to decide the policy of their country, would walk back and forth on the steep path of the castle park, discussing their theories and plans for Sweden's future. "He was very good at straightening out problems and finding solutions in differences of opinion," his brother Sten said of him.

There had been many students discussing many theories since the University was founded in 1477. Once social injustice and inequality were taken for granted, and the talk of the students was about ancient times in Rome and Greece or the life hereafter. But gradually, through the long procession of years, their thoughts had turned to the present and the near future, and the welfare of all alike.

As the school year drew to a close, the students began looking forward to their most joyful celebration. Textbooks and lecture notes were put aside and they prepared to welcome the coming of spring. On the last day of April, wearing their white caps, they gathered in front of the University Library and waited for the stroke of three. This was a signal for them to go racing in a mad

dash down the hill to the town below. It was like seeing a
river in spring flood to look from above on this mass of
white-capped, running students. When the University
was new, the students had fought mock battles on horse-
back, one side taking the part of Winter and the other,
Summer. And Summer always won. Now, instead of
mock battles, there was dancing in the street, with music
played by the student band.

At sundown, May fires were lit in scattered places on
the Uppland plain. The air was filled with the pungent
smell of burning wood, and from all directions curls of
smoke rose up to become lost in the blue night sky. The
old bell in the wooden tower beside the castle rang the
curfew hour at nine o'clock, but there'd be no sleeping
for the students on this night. They marched back up
the hill to gather around the bell tower. There speeches
were made, welcoming the coming of spring, and the
student choir led in the singing of spring songs.

The castle doors were thrown open for this occasion. A
banquet was held in one of the great tower rooms, with
row after row of long tables laden with food. Agnes
Hammarskjöld, warm and vivacious, enjoyed the
young people, with their laughter and song bringing
new life to the old castle. And her husband, with all his
dignity, did not forget that he, too, in his student days,
had worn the white cap and danced all night. Now Dag,
the last of his sons still a student, was taking part with his
friends of Uppsala Nation. Sometimes on these nights
Dag led his companions on explorations through winding
passages of the castle, from tower to dungeon.

After the banquet, there was dancing again, which lasted until morning, when the May sun rose above the plain's horizon. Walpurgis Night was over. The witches had flown on magpie wings to the mountaintops and had danced away the winter snows. Light had conquered Darkness. Good had triumphed over Evil.

This was not the end of the celebration. The first of May brought a new day for feasting and dancing, and songs of spring, and the summer's sun. It was only a beginning of a series of festivities which went on until the end of the month, when the school year came to an end, degrees were given and the summer vacation began.

Dag would always love the Swedish summers. His brother Bo had taken him on his first mountain climb when he was seventeen, the year he took his entrance examinations to the University. There was never a summer afterward that he did not start out with a knapsack on his back, a camera over his shoulder, and a book in his pocket. Sometimes he went with a friend, but as often as not he was alone. He called the mountains of Scandinavia harmonious rather than dramatic. Climbing them, he said, called for endurance rather than balance and struggle. He walked with long strides up the gentle slopes, and he stepped over rocks and crevices with a sureness of foot won by practice.

He searched in hidden places for rare plants and flowers as he had done when he was a child. And when he came to a turn of the trail overlooking a splendid view, he took out his camera to photograph it. He would stretch out on the sloping ground to rest, with a cup of coffee poured from a thermos jar and a book he had brought along.

Though his studies at the University were on political economy, he kept up the interest in literature of his undergraduate days. He had his father's gift for languages, and he read the works of his favorite authors in their original language. He read Thomas Mann in German and Joseph Conrad in English. He had been disappointed in the type of literature he had been expected to read when he began to study French, and he mentioned this to Mrs. Söderblom.

"I thought I'd be reading about the progress of ideas through the ages, and not waste time on love affairs of the authors," he said.

"Have you tried Pascal?" Mrs. Söderblom asked.

Blaise Pascal, who lived over three hundred years ago, was one of the greatest mathematicians and physicists of his time, but he is best known now by his one small book of thoughts, *Pensées*. From the first reading the book became a constant companion to Dag.

"We do not content ourselves with the life we have in ourselves and in our own being; we desire to live an imaginary life in the mind of others, and for this purpose we desire to shine. We labor endlessly to adorn this imaginary existence and neglect the real."

This book led to others of the same type, *The Imitation of Christ*, by Thomas à Kempis, *Meditations* of Marcus Aurelius, the philosophy of Thomas Aquinas. "You cannot know everything. But you can check your arrogance, rise superior to pleasures or pains, spurn reputation, keep your temper with the stupid and the ingrate. Yes, you can even care for them," the Roman Emperor Marcus Aurelius had written to himself centuries ago.

Dag read these words which were the musings of a man with his soul. He began about that time putting down his own thoughts which he was to call negotiations with himself and with God. Sometimes he expressed himself in poetry or a parable. Sometimes there was a single line, a reminder to himself or an admonition. Or, like Thomas à Kempis, he wrote of loneliness and meditations on death.

"What you have to attempt—to be yourself," he wrote when he was not yet thirty. "What you have to pray for—to become a mirror in which, according to the degree of purity of heart you have attained, the greatness of life will be reflected."

THREE

1925–1948

In the rose garden and along the arcades of the Sigtuna Foundation close to Uppsala, Dag Hammarskjöld could be seen often on a fair day, strolling with a textbook in his hand. He had decided to work for a law degree to prepare himself better for a career in public service. As he read, his face had the calm expression of one who had taught himself to concentrate and retain the meaning of the text. Sometimes he would pause long enough to glance through the window where a young friend was writing his first novel.

"How many pages have you made up today?" he would ask teasingly.

To the writer, Sven Stolpe, the study of law seemed a drab thing for one who had a B.A. degree in literature and was working on a doctorate in economics. He felt pity for young Hammarskjöld.

"But I found that he was in no way oppressed or burdened by all that dead material. His soul lived on beside it, lively and untrammeled," he wrote.

When they first met, Stolpe was impressed by the young man's courteous manner, and his understanding and integrity. He predicted in his diary at that time that Dag Hammarskjöld would become prime minister of Sweden while he was still young.

Stolpe was deeply religious at a time when many of the students of Uppsala were skeptics and wanted to change the old order of Church as well as State. He was amazed to find a student of law and economics also interested in the writings of saints and mystics. They took walks together discussing Pascal, Thomas à Kempis, Péguy. Through Stolpe, Dag Hammarskjöld discovered the Spanish poet and mystic, St. John of the Cross. He read the short poem, written almost four hundred years before, "Song of the Soul Delighted by the Knowledge of God," with the refrain "though it be night" recurring throughout. And the line "faith is the union of God with the soul" he would repeat often in later years.

The friendship that developed between the two young men through their common interests was a sincere and lasting one, but, like the friendships of Dag's childhood, it was never close.

"To a person of any observation, it was clear that he carried an inner world within him to whose echoes he listened eagerly, but about which he seldom found opportunity to speak," Stolpe said of him.

Another friend of that period, Per Olof Ekelöf, wrote of his walks and talks with Hammarskjöld as a young

student: "We promenaded up and down the streets for
hours or went out into the countryside, talking enthusi-
astically the whole time. We read the same novels and
poetry, compared our reactions to them and analyzed
them closely. Science, politics, philosophical questions—
we went into everything."

Sometimes in summer they went on a camping trip to
Lapland. Dag loved the desolate, magnificent country
which Linnaeus had explored long ago. The two friends
tramped over the high moorlands and crossed swift
glacier streams, and at night they pitched their tent in
some sheltered spot. They could go days in that region
without seeing a human being, or a sign of human
habitation.

"But we brought Uppsala with us out into the wilderness," Ekelöf wrote. "Talking all the time, we tramped
along with some mountain peak as our reference point. In
the ardour of our youth we were less interested in each
other than in what we were talking about."

Ekelöf spoke of himself as an atheist then, but he felt
shy and out of his element in the presence of Dag's
idealism, and the subject of religion was never touched
upon between them.

A year and a half after starting the law course,
young Hammarskjöld received his degree. At that time,
1930, his father, approaching his seventieth year, decided to retire from his post as lord lieutenant of Uppland. Dag was the only one of the sons still living at
home then, and when his parents left the old Vasa Castle
to move to Stockholm, he went with them. They took an

apartment in a building owned by the Nobel Foundation facing the Humblegarden, a large park surrounding the Royal Library.

For a brief time Dag Hammarskjöld was a lecturer at the Stockholm University, until he received an appointment as secretary of the Royal Commission on Unemployment. At the same time he was working on his doctorate in economics. The report he wrote for the Commission, dealing with inflations and depressions, served also as his doctoral dissertation. It was two hundred and sixty-six printed pages which he had written at the rate of four pages a day. Those who heard him read it called it subtle, involved, and very learned, but he ended it with a quotation from *Alice in Wonderland:* "That's nothing to what I could say if I chose."

As secretary of the Unemployment Commission, Hammarskjöld called in a group of young economists near his own age. Some had been among those fellow students at Uppsala who had so fervently discussed their theories of social reform. They were not so much influenced by Karl Marx as by the English economist, John Maynard Keynes.

Keynes was opposed to government ownership of industry, and he believed that a man should be allowed to choose or change his job, buy or sell goods, and earn a respectable profit. But some of his theories would seem more radical than those of Marx to the older economists. They held the theory that, in times of depression, the government should balance its budget by raising taxes and reducing spending. Keynes argued that a country could lift itself out of a depression only through lower taxes, higher interests, and heavy government spending. But merely spending for temporary relief was not enough. The money should go for durable things, such as housing, public utilities, and transportation. Employers who lowered wages and discharged large numbers of their workers only added to a depression, and the same was true of bankers who raised the rate of interest when savings fell off.

Sweden was still feeling the effects of the 1929 Wall Street crash, followed by low wages and unemployment when, in 1932, the country had a crisis of its own in the Kreuger scandal. When Ivar Kreuger, head of the company that controlled more than half the world's production of matches, shot himself in Paris, it was discovered that his accounts had been falsified and his assets and profits recorded were on paper only. With this disclosure of corruption within one of Sweden's leading private industries, many other industries went bankrupt. There was a change of government after this, with the Social Democrats taking over. This called for practical measures instead of mere theories on economics.

The work Dag Hammarskjöld was doing with the Unemployment Commission won him the confidence of Social Democrat Ernst Wigforss, who became Finance Minister in the new government. Hammarskjöld was made assistant to the head of the government-owned Bank of Sweden and principal clerk in the finance department. Before he was thirty, there was a change in the finance department, and the post of Permanent Secretary was vacant. Wigforss wanted this to go to young Hammarskjöld, but there was some question as to whether such responsibility should go to one so young. Some talked of dividing the post, having two permanent secretaries instead of one. Hammarskjöld, as he often did, went to his father for advice.

"All or nothing," the father said firmly.

Dag, like his father, took no interest in party politics, and he did not become a member of any of the parties. The first duty of a civil servant, he believed, was that he serve the community and not any group, party, or political interests.

"He was a patriot without parading it, regarding it as something to be taken for granted," Ekelöf wrote of him.

Bo was at that time Under-Secretary in the Ministry of Social Welfare, though he, too, had not joined the party. Some wondered how Hjalmar Hammarskjöld felt at having two of his sons working under a Social Democratic government, but Dag insisted that his father was no defender of privilege. He spoke of him as a reformist, though one of conservative disposition.

"I am a conservative person," Bo declared. "As a conservative person I can serve my country best by working for social reforms. The country belongs to the people, and they should feel a part in its welfare."

The two brothers were responsible for many of the reforms brought about by the Social Democrats. Most of the credit for ending Sweden's unemployment during the depression went to Dag. He saw, through his work at the State Bank, how the theory of Keynes could be applied practically.

He worked with tireless energy. It was as if some unseen force were driving him, warning him that time was short and many lifetimes must be crowded into one. But no matter how busy the day, he took time to have dinner and spend a few hours in the evening with his parents. He closed his office at six, sometimes stopping to buy flowers for his mother, and he smiled indulgently when she urged him not to work so hard, or to wear his muffler and button his overcoat against the cold. At nine o'clock, his parents' bedtime, he returned to his office when there was unfinished work waiting for him. Many a time, late at night, when the massive gray government buildings were hidden in darkness, one lone light could be seen shining from a window of the Finance Department. There, undisturbed by committee meetings or visitors, or the ring of the telephone, Dag Hammarskjöld worked on without thinking of the time. When the work was unusually heavy or urgent, he was joined by some of the members of his staff. They worked until about eleven, then they went to a small restaurant in the old part of the city close to the government buildings. There they relaxed over a pot of tea and talked about books or music or philosophy until midnight, when they returned to their work refreshed.

The Hammarskjölds' good friend, Archbishop Söderblom, had died in 1931, a year after he won the Nobel Peace Prize, and was buried with the great men of Sweden's past in the Uppsala Cathedral. Six years later the Hammarskjöld family had a more personal loss in the death of Åke, the second of the four brothers, of rheumatic fever. It was at a time when the world was again faced with the threat of war. Both the Peace Conference at The Hague and the League of Nations for which Åke had worked, proved powerless against it.

In September, 1939, Germany declared war on Poland, and as in the previous war, one country after another came into the fight. Sweden was again faced with the problem of keeping neutral in a belligerent world. This war was brought closer when, in the spring of 1940, Germany invaded Norway, Denmark, Belgium, and Holland. The year brought a greater sadness to Dag Hammarskjöld in the death of his mother. Her body was taken back to Uppsala to be buried in the quiet, shady cemetery close by the University.

Hjalmar Hammarskjöld, nearing eighty, was still mentally alert and had good advice for his sons when they came to him for it. But he had grown more and more retiring. "Like a block of Småland granite," a friend of Dag's described him. When visitors came, he quietly went back to his study, asking to be excused because of his age and infirmities. His days were spent reading books, sent him by the Swedish Academy, to be considered for the Nobel Prize. From his window he could look down on the park across the street and watch the seasons come and go, the melting pools of snow in spring, the mock orange in summer bloom perfuming the air around, and the jackdaws flitting in and out among the trees in autumn. He smiled at their senseless fighting

Young Dag Hammarskjöld with his mother Agnes Hammarskjöld and his older brother Sten.

Dag Hammarskjöld was about ten years old when he and his mother posed for this picture.

Dag at sixteen.

A formal portrait made about 1926.

and said it was like the behavior of people. They brought back memories of the jackdaws that swarmed about the spires and towers of the Cathedral and the castle where he had lived. He called them messengers from Uppsala. Dag, who knew he spoke in loneliness, said he was one who had been placed entirely aside. The father himself spoke about the extravagance of life that was constantly discarding the experience built up over long years, only to push it aside and in the end destroy it by old age and death. But each generation has its own task, and now the sons were following the same path he and his fathers before him had taken, and were building up experiences of their own.

Though the war was carried to Sweden's borders on the south, east, and west, the country succeeded in remaining neutral. But with foreign trade cut off, there were shortages of food and raw material, and a threat of inflation. Lights burned long in the somber gray government buildings, and more than likely the last one that was turned off was where Dag Hammarskjöld had been at work. He was made chairman of the governors of the Bank of Sweden, with new duties added to those of the Finance Department. He established price controls to prevent inflation, planned the country's economy for the war years and afterward, and conferred with the governments-in-exile about financial aid they would be needing.

As busy as his days were, Dag Hammarskjöld had a way of organizing his time so that there were precious periods of leisure. The theater or a concert relaxed him, or he could spend an evening listening to recordings of his favorite music: Bach, Mahler, Stravinsky. He also made it a rule to set aside one hour of the day at least for reading.

On Fridays, when the day's work was over and there was nothing urgent to keep him over the weekend, he took a train out of Stockholm with a few companions or alone, to go bicycling or hiking or mountain climbing. Once on a mountain slope he recited to the friends with him the whole of T. S. Eliot's long poem, "The Hollow Men." Here on this tranquil spot, high about the world's confusions, the bickerings of men and nations were as senseless as the fighting of jackdaws his father spoke about.

> We are the hollow men
> We are the stuffed men
> Leaning together
> Headpiece filled with straw, Alas!

Wherever he went on his excursions, whether to the Lapland wilderness or to the gentle province Skåne in the southern part of Sweden, he was reminded of some poem or passage of prose describing the place. Swedish writers, from Linnaeus to those of the present day, have loved the landscape of their country. They write of summer in the plains under a burning sun, with trickling ditches and jubilant larks falling like drops in space. And they write of the coming of spring in Lapland, with the violet-blue shine of brushwood and the tree trunks stiffened as if in a weird dance, casting pale-blue shadows on the snow.

During the war years the people of Sweden, isolated from the rest of Europe and struggling to keep from being drawn into the fighting, felt more closely drawn to their own country, its history, its folkways, and its landscape. Hammarskjöld thought there should be a book giving a picture of the country through these fragments of Swedish literature, both poetry and prose. He took time out to help with the editing. The book was published by the Swedish Travel Association, an organization whose motto was "Know your country." Dag Hammarskjöld, long a member of the organization, did not include his own poetic descriptions of sunlight and the caroling of larks blended into one cool ecstasy, of yellow birches of Lapland trembling in the storm, and of the rain-laden east wind rushing down the dried-up river bed. No one knew of the pages of writing hidden in his desk drawer.

The war lasted for five years, and the peace that followed was no real peace. Countries were divided. Alliances were shifted. Former allies became enemies, and former enemies became friends.

"The greatest prayer of man does not ask for victory, but for peace," a Swedish writer said.

Before the war had drawn to a close, representatives of forty-six nations held a conference in San Francisco and drew up the Charter of the United Nations for the maintenance of international peace and security. The begin-

ning paragraphs of the Charter expressed the highest
ideals of man :

We, the Peoples of the United Nations, Determined
    to save succeeding generations from the scourge of
war, which twice in our lifetime has brought untold
sorrow to mankind, and
    to reaffirm faith in fundamental human rights, in
the dignity and worth of the human person, in equal
rights of men and women and of nations large and small,
and
    to establish conditions under which justice and re-
spect for the obligations arising from treaties and other
sources of international law can be maintained, and
    to promote social progress and better standards of
life in larger freedom.

The Hammarskjöld brothers and their father must
have often discussed the reports about this new organization, and compared its aims with the earlier ones
working for peace. Dag felt that the failure to prevent
the Second World War was not the fault of the League of
Nations. The nations themselves had failed because they
had not lived up to their pledged word. But the ideals of
the old organization had been hard to live up to. Its
founders had dreamed of a new heaven while the greatest
hope of the United Nations was to be permitted to save
this old earth, he said in a later speech.

The first General Assembly of the United Nations
opened in London in January, 1946, five months after
the end of the war. The following April the League of

Nations closed its work and turned over its assets to the
United Nations.

That summer a crowd of pilgrims gathered at the
basilica of the Madeleine at Vezelay, in the center of
France, to pray for peace and for forgiveness of the
world's sin of war and destruction. There were men from
all walks of life: doctors, carpenters, bankers, teachers,
and janitors. They had come on foot, walking through
France in the hot sun from village to village. There were
fourteen groups, merging from all directions—from
England, Switzerland, Austria, Luxembourg, Belgium,
and from all parts of France, each group carrying a
heavy oak cross. They walked up the last hill in bare
feet. There, one by one, the crosses were planted and a
beacon fire was lit to announce the arrival of each group.

They camped on the hilltop facing a huge wooden
cross. It marked the site where, on an Easter Sunday
eight hundred years before, St. Bernard had preached to
King Louis VII and a hundred thousand barons, knights,
and squires starting out on the Second Crusade. Now in
the gathering darkness the modern pilgrims knelt around
the crosses to pray and wait. Suddenly the bells rang
out triumphantly and the basilica shone with floodlights
inside and out. The lights beamed on one of the crosses in
such a way that the kneeling pilgrims, looking up, saw a
perfectly formed shadow of a cross standing out dark
against a light cloudbank.

"Behold, how good and how pleasant it is for brethren
to dwell together in unity."

Dag Hammarskjöld was deeply impressed by the

story of the modern pilgrims. He would remember it long after and half a world away, when he saw Buddhist priests in the Himalayas preparing for a pilgrimage.

The war had brought suffering to all of Europe, not only to the defeated nations but to the victors as well. The nightmare of destruction was over—the slaughter of innocent people because of their faith, the use of the new and terrifying atomic weapon, the blackouts and the dread screech of the siren before the bombs fell. But there was a staggering amount of rebuilding to be done. The economy of Europe was on the verge of collapse and the people faced starvation and desperation.

Though Sweden had formed no alliances and had succeeded in keeping out of the war, she was faced with the problem of adjusting to a peacetime economy with the rest of Europe. Dag Hammarskjöld had left the Finance Department and was now envoy and financial expert to the Foreign Department. As chairman of the Bank of Sweden, he had much of the responsibility of holding off a postwar inflation and in keeping wages stable. He also carried on trade negotiations for much needed raw materials.

Heavy loans from the United States to the suffering countries had brought only temporary relief. In 1947, a new offer to save Europe from ruin was made under the Marshall Plan. Financial aid on a much larger scale would be given over a period of four years on the condition that the nations receiving it would do their utmost in helping themselves and helping each other toward becoming self-supporting.

The Organization for European Economic Cooperation was set up to prepare the way for the loans. The countries that were to take part sent representatives to Paris to discuss how the funds should be allotted, and see that the nations receiving aid were doing as much as possible for each other.

Sweden became a member, not as a country that had suffered war damage, but to help in the recovery of Europe as a whole. Young Hammarskjöld was chosen to head the Swedish delegation. With his knowledge of languages he was able to understand what the delegates from other countries said and so make his reply without the need of an interpreter. He was made vice-chairman of the executive committee, and it was not long before he became known as one who could speak calmly no matter how heated the discussion. Many of the member nations wanted as large a share as they could get of the American money. Their demands piled up until they came to more than the amount available for all. Hammarskjöld was the one who could be relied upon to reason with each side in a dispute and find a solution that was just to all. Other delegates did not always agree with him, but they respected him for his sense of justice and integrity.

He spent the year 1948 in Paris with the European Economic Organization, returning to Stockholm each weekend to make his report and to see his aging father. While in Paris, he kept the same tireless work schedule that he had in Stockholm. There were the long evening sessions of the executive committee, with a pause perhaps for the theater or opera or discussions in some quiet restaurant, then a return to work until a late hour. If there was some free time during the week, he and the other Swedish delegates went on an excursion outside of Paris, to Chartres, Reims, and to Vezelay where the pilgrims had prayed for peace.

At the start of the Marshall Plan, the money was meant for economic recovery only; not one cent was to be spent for military purposes. It was the start of an international cooperation in which countries worked together for the good of all. Recommendations were approved to build dikes in Holland, to drain malarial swamps in Sardinia, to build steel mills in France and railroads in Turkey.

The rift between the Soviet bloc and the Western countries had been steadily growing. At the time of the Paris meetings, Russia put up a rail blockade against West Berlin. Western planes, at the rate of one every three minutes, flew in food and fuel for almost a year, until the blockade was lifted.

Five European countries—Britain, France, Belgium, Holland, and Luxembourg—signed a treaty pledging military aid from all if one of them came under attack. Later they were joined by the United States, Canada, Portugal, Italy, and three of the Scandinavian countries: Norway, Denmark, and Iceland. They formed the North Atlantic Treaty Organization, with the agreement that an armed attack against one would be considered an attack against all.

Sweden was urged to join, but the country kept neutral as it had during two world wars and would not

become a part of this alliance. Like the elder Hammarskjöld during the First World War, Dag cooperated with
the West, but at the same time he insisted upon honoring
Sweden's trade agreements with Russia.

He wrote an article which he called "To Choose Europe," in which he, as a neutral individual within a
neutral country, explained Sweden's stand. In a dispute
between nations, he said, the solution should come
through the use of international law.

FOUR

1949–1952

After his return from Paris, Hammarskjöld was made Cabinet Secretary in the Foreign Department, and in 1951 he was appointed Vice-Minister of Foreign Affairs. He became the sixteenth member of the Swedish cabinet and the only one who was not a member of the Social Democratic party. His duties were to assist the Foreign Minister, Östen Unden in economic affairs of international interest.

Hammarskjöld could look back on the twenty years he had served his government with some satisfaction in what had been accomplished. With the rest of Europe, Sweden had brought her economy back to normal. Production was up, and the foreign exchange and credit standing good. Social reforms were put into effect and the country, along with Denmark and Norway, was on its way to becoming a model welfare state. The goal was to wipe out illiteracy and dire poverty.

There were now nine years of compulsory education with free tuition from kindergarten through college. Each child, up to the age of sixteen, received an annual cash grant from the government; and for those still in school at sixteen and seventeen, there was a monthly income to help them complete their education. The sick were given all medicines they needed, free care in hospital wards, and two-thirds of their doctors' fees. For the old and disabled, there were pensions amounting to two-thirds of the annual income during their fifteen best-paid years. Labor leaders were chosen from among educated men whose concern was for the welfare of the workers rather than for power. The unions worked in harmony with industry, and strikes were rare.

Many of the conservatives criticized Dag Hammarskjöld for remaining so long with a government that was growing more and more radical. In the year he became a member of the Swedish cabinet, he wrote an article for a Social Democrat magazine explaining his stand. The ideal civil servant was politically independent, so he wrote, one who was his own party, who had a definite personal scale of values, and who felt one should be free to try what one thought was right. As for himself, he said, he had a scale of moral values that did not fit into the frame of any of the parties. He had adopted the philosophy of Albert Schweitzer.

In another article Hammarskjöld again mentioned Schweitzer's influence on his own thinking. He had in-

herited from generations of soldiers and government officials on his father's side a belief that no life was more
satisfactory than one of selfless devotion to one's country or to humanity—a service that required a sacrifice
of all personal interests and a courage to stand up for
one's convictions. From the scholars and clergymen on
his mother's side, he inherited a belief that all men were
equals as children of God.

"The two ideals which dominated my childhood
world met me fully harmonized and adjusted to the
demands of our world today in the ethics of Albert
Schweitzer," he wrote.

He felt a restlessness at that time which he could not
explain. He was forty-six and it seemed that all his
years until then had been spent in preparation. But
preparation for what? He had gone far in his career as a
public servant, as far as one could go and still keep out of
party politics. But he knew that life had some other
purpose than this for him.

One day at lunch with Gunnar Myrdal, a fellow
economist, he gave some hint of this restlessness. Myrdal
described him as breezy, cordial, yet disciplined as he
mentioned a few of the careers he might follow—such as
a lord lieutenant as his father had been. When his
companion suggested he become a writer, Hammarskjöld
only smiled as if to say this was not what he had in
mind at all.

"What I ask for is absurd: that life shall have a
meaning," he wrote in his journal. "What I strive for is
impossible: that my life shall acquire a meaning. I dare

not believe, I do not see how I shall ever be able to believe: that I am not alone."

He wrote often of his loneliness that year, and of a sense of waiting, as if for some message that failed to come: "Pray that your loneliness may spur you into finding something to live for, great enough to die for."

During a quiet week of June, 1952, Hammarskjöld set out alone for Lapland. He knew this last great wilderness of Europe in all its seasons. He knew the long midwinter nights when the sun appeared briefly on the horizon only to sink again, and the loneliness of the isolated people fighting an uneven battle against cold and poverty. He had heard the call of wild geese in spring coming in to their nesting places, and he had seen them in autumn with necks outstretched, following the leader in their flight south. Now in June, when the day never dies, the summer sun brought out the vegetation in almost tropical splendor for its brief blooming. A feeling of peace came over him as always when he was in a wild and lonely place, walking along overgrown and deserted roads or climbing the lone, zigzag mountain trails.

The peace was shattered by the arrival of a military plane sent to take him back to Stockholm. The Russians had shot down a Swedish plane over the Baltic Sea on Friday. Again, on Sunday, the plane sent out to search for survivors was shot down. Foreign Minister Unden was on vacation in Italy, and no one other than Dag Hammarskjöld had the authority to act. He immediately flew back to the capital and, still dressed for mountain climbing, rushed to his office to take over.

An exchange of notes followed. It was an anxious time for a country that had managed to keep at peace for so many generations. The Russian notes always arrived at a late hour. It soon became obvious to Hammarskjöld that they had planned it so that their message would reach Sweden in time for the morning newspaper but too late for the Foreign Ministry to act. It became a kind of game with him and his aides to outwit the Russians. Their office was kept open, with someone on watch, until the message came through, or they were sure there'd be no message that night.

The members of NATO followed these events with interest, hoping that now Sweden would be persuaded to join, but the country still insisted on keeping neutral.

Hammarskjöld had gathered together a group of outstanding young men as his aides in the Foreign Office. Some had worked with him on the European Economic Organization and they continued to work in harmony together. Myrdal said of him that toward his colleagues he was full of kind and generous good will, and that he had an incredible ability to lead and instill enthusiasm so that even the insignificant achieved what was beyond their normal capacity.

Since the end of the war, Dag Hammarskjöld had been living alone. He had taken a seven-room apartment on the top floor of an old-fashioned brick building a short walking distance from his father's place. His windows looked across a narrow street upon Sture Park, where there were trees as old and gnarled as at the castle park in Uppsala. He entertained friends occasionally, those who worked in government service with him, and the artists and writers he knew.

Among his friends, the closest, perhaps, was the artist Bo Beskow. He also enjoyed being with Uno Willers, the Royal Librarian, Karl Gierow, director of the Royal Dramatic Theater, and his aides in the Foreign Department, Per Lind, Leif Belfrage, and Sven Backlund. He liked sharing with them the things that gave him pleasure—a hike in the country, a recording of a Bach concerto, a favorite book.

"I've read many books on philosophy and modern poetry I would have overlooked except for him," his former chief Wigforss said.

He had plans to translate into Swedish some of the works he had especially enjoyed. Among them was the poetry of St.-John Perse who had become known only since the end of the war. Perse, like Hammarskjöld, came from a well-to-do aristocratic family. He had trained for government service and became France's Permanent Secretary of Foreign Affairs. When France was invaded by the Germans in 1940, he fled to America, where he spent the war years. Both men were sensitive, reserved, and found release from the problems of their work through poetry. "My name does not belong to letters," Perse once stated. In spite of that, he became better known as a poet than as a diplomat and eventually resigned from government service so he could live quietly and devote his full time to writing.

Dag Hammarskjöld, on the other hand, wrote in secret as a man prays in secret. During his lifetime, only one person, and that was Leif Belfrage who worked with him in the Foreign Office, would know of the existence of his private journals. But not even Belfrage knew the contents: "God does not die on the day when we cease to believe in a personal deity, but we die on the day when our lives cease to be illumined by the steady radiance, renewed daily, of a wonder, the source of which is beyond all reason."

Once, when reading a book of history, the thought came to him that problems which had once seemed so vital were really quite simple. It was just that they were not understood at the time. Now, looking back on them from a distance of years, they had become nothing more than cold abstractions. He found himself substituting names of living people for the names of those long dead. "We appear as rather stupid, foolish, self-seeking puppets, moved by obvious strings which now and again get tangled up," he wrote. It seemed proof to him that all was vanity.

Another year passed. "Soon comes the night," Dag Hammarskjöld wrote at the beginning of 1953. "For all that has been—Thanks! To all that shall be—Yes!"

Maturity was, among other things, to live up to one's best, he observed. And goodness was something so simple: "always to live for others, never to seek one's own advantage."

As Vice-Minister of Foreign Affairs, he often had to go on trips abroad. For a brief time, early in 1953, he went to New York with the Swedish delegation to the United Nations. In the vast Assembly Hall the delegates took the places assigned them in alphabetical order according to the name of their country. This place, immense yet simple in design, had an atmosphere of tranquillity when it was empty; but filled with delegates of all the member nations, there was a tension and bitterness unknown to the old League of Nations.

A harassed Secretary-General, Trygve Lie of Norway, sat at the right of the General Assembly president, on a raised platform facing the delegates. He had announced his resignation a few months before and was staying on only until a successor could be found. On one side, he was accused by a United States congressional committee of having American Communists on his staff. On the other side, the Soviet Union had boycotted him and had refused to recognize him for the past year and a half because of his approval to sending United Nations troops to fight in the Korean War. The armistice in Korea was being held up until a settlement could be reached on the exchange of war prisoners. About a fourth of the North Korean and Chinese prisoners were refusing to return to their homeland and what they felt would be certain death. There was also the problem of choosing a Secretary-General to succeed Trygve Lie. Every candidate that had been proposed so far had been turned down by one nation or another in the Security Council, and there seemed no prospect of an agreement.

There were sharp exchanges of words and long propaganda speeches in many languages, picked up in the glass-enclosed booths on the side walls by interpreters, broadcasters, and television equipment, and sent around

the world. The United Nations then was close to going
the way of the League of Nations. A listener at that
Seventh Session of the General Assembly might have
reflected on the words of the Charter: "to practice tolerance and live together in peace with one another as good
neighbors, and to unite our strength to maintain international peace and security . . ." and have wondered
what had happened to the dream that inspired them.

The Swedish delegation was scarcely noticed at this
Assembly session. Sweden was a small country, had no
colonies, no claim on other territory, and no neighboring
country was claiming Swedish territory. So there were
no problems to bring up for discussion.

Sven Backlund, who had been with the Foreign Ministry and was now with the Swedish Embassy in Washington, came up to New York to spend a day with
Hammarskjöld. They walked along the city streets and
stopped in a restaurant as they had enjoyed doing in
Stockholm, discussing the topic on everybody's mind—
the successor to Trygve Lie. The candidates from
Canada, from the Philippines, from Belgium, India, and
Thailand, had all been rejected. Since Lie was a Norwegian, it was not likely that another Scandinavian
would be chosen, yet Swedish Ambassador Eric Boheman's name had been mentioned as a possibility. After a
few weeks in New York, Hammarskjöld left the Swedish
delegation and returned to his duties in Stockholm.

The Bank of Sweden had commissioned Bo Beskow to
paint a portrait of the former Chairman of the Board.
With the vivacious Beskow, his opposite in temperament,

Hammarskjöld felt more relaxed than with any of his friends. In the last week of March, he was at the artist's studio for a sitting. The snow was still on the ground and the air was sharp and cold as in winter, but under the snow the ground was stirring, with here and there a gray patch of earth in a place that had caught the sun. The first wave of warm air would bring the starlings, wagtails, and bullfinches, and suddenly it would be spring.

The two men were discussing Dag Hammarskjöld's trip to New York and the United Nations, and the subject came up of a candidate for Secretary-General that all could agree upon.

"It occurs to me that you would be just the right man for the job," Bo Beskow said suddenly.

Hammarskjöld brushed the idea aside.

"No one has been crazy enough to ask me, nor would I be crazy enough to accept," he replied.

At about the same time, in New York, this same idea had occurred to the representative from France, Hoppenot, who had worked with Hammarskjöld on the Economic Committee. Stalin had died on the fifth of March, and the Russian delegates were in a subdued mood. When Dag Hammarskjöld's name was proposed at a meeting of the Security Council on March 31, no objections were made. The vote in his favor was ten to one. Only Formosa China abstained, this because Sweden recognized Red China.

The first hint of this action that came to Hammarskjöld was in a cable from the Swedish delegation in New

York, saying that he was being mentioned as a possible candidate. He couldn't take this seriously, for only a short while ago he had been at the General Assembly meetings and no one had spoken to him about it. He thought it was some practical joke. Late that night when he was alone in his apartment, the telephone began ringing. One news service after another called to tell him he had been chosen by the Security Council, and they wanted to know if he had a statement to make. Hammarskjöld remarked to one of the callers, an editor he knew, that if the news had come the next day, April 1, he might have understood. Even then, he added, it would have been a cruel kind of joke.

The next day a cable came from the president of the Security Council, Dr. Bokhari of Pakistan, with the official news that he had been nominated. "In view of the immense importance of this post," the message continued, "especially at the present time, the members of the Security Council express the earnest hope that you will agree to accept the appointment if, as they hope and believe, it is shortly made by the General Assembly."

Dag Hammarskjöld took the news to his father, and he also telephoned Foreign Secretary Unden who was on a short vacation in Capri. Both men agreed that he should accept. Then followed a busy day making preparations. He cabled his decision to the Security Council: "With a strong feeling of insufficiency, I hesitate to accept the candidature, but I do not feel that I should refuse the task imposed upon me should the Assembly follow the recommendation of the Security Council, by which I am deeply honored."

After that, he held his first press conference. Seated at a long table, surrounded by newsmen and photographers, he apologized for his attitude of the night before. He had heard nothing about his nomination until the telephone began ringing in the middle of the night, he explained. He had returned from New York and Washington only two weeks before and in neither place had there been a word about his being considered. He seemed in good spirits and answered questions willingly enough, but he warned them there was little he could say. He felt neither optimistic nor pessimistic about his chances for success. From what one could read in the newspapers, there would be difficulties to face. One could only do one's best in such a job.

In spite of all there was to do, Dag Hammarskjöld kept his appointment for a sitting with Bo Beskow, but the artist was in no mood for painting. He poured glasses of sherry and the two friends sat talking—Beskow exuberant, but Hammarskjöld quiet, contemplative.

"I must accept," he said. "It is a matter of duty, and I have no other choice."

Alone in the night, he wrote: "When in decisive moments—as now—God acts, it is with a stern purposefulness, a Sophoclean irony. When the hour strikes, He takes what is His. What have *you* to say?—Your prayer had been answered, as you know. God has a use for you, even though what He asks doesn't happen to suit you at the moment. God, who 'abases him whom He raises up.' "

Word came on April 7 that the General Assembly had met and affirmed the nomination of Dag Hammarskjöld as Secretary-General of the United Nations. On that same day Hammarskjöld copied in his journal a quotation from Thomas Aquinas: "Their lives grounded in and sustained by God, they are incapable of any kind of pride; because they give back to God all the benefits He has bestowed on them, they do not glorify each other, but do all things to the glory of God alone."

The Swedish cabinet met and consented to Hammarskjöld's release. Hammarskjöld then called on the king to take his leave and had a long talk with him. He made arrangements for Per Lind, one of his able aides in the Foreign Office, to become a member of his staff at the United Nations. Sweden's Ambassador Boheman flew back to Sweden to accompany Hammarskjöld to New York, and there were conferences with him.

In the midst of this pressure, he took time out to go to Uppsala, where he visited his mother's grave and called on his old friend, Mrs. Söderblom. The old castle on the hill brought back memories of his childhood and youth, the search for spotted daffodils or a death's head butterfly, the carriage rides in the country at midsummer, and the gay Walpurgis Night festivals to welcome the spring. There had been sleigh rides and student dances, and a young woman, brilliant, sparkling, beautiful. There had also been the dreams and the ideals that come to a youth with the sureness of a call that would be too strong to resist. In his student days, here in Uppsala, he had written:

Smiling, sincere, incorruptible—
His body disciplined and limber.

A man who had become what he could,
And was what he was—
Ready at any moment to gather everything
Into one simple sacrifice.

Now that he was forty-eight, the call had come. It was not at the time nor in the way he had expected, but he was ready to answer "Yes."

"To be free, to be able to stand up and leave *everything* behind—without looking back. To say *Yes*—"

FIVE

1953–1955

On the ninth of April, 1953, four days after Easter, a Scandinavian Airlines plane landed at Idlewild in New York. The crowd gathered at the airport terminal saw a slender, sandy-haired man step out, looking much younger than his forty-eight years. He was poised, self-assured, yet he had a look of slight bewilderment at the sight of the many newsmen and photographers pressing toward him.

Trygve Lie, who had been Secretary-General of the United Nations since its beginning, stepped forward to welcome his successor. He wished him luck and happiness, but he warned, "You are taking over the world's most impossible job." He then introduced Dag Hammarskjöld to the waiting newsmen.

Hammarskjöld apologized for having so little to say at his first press conference on American soil. For one reason, he said, he wanted to do a job and not

72

talk about it—not even afterward—much less in advance. He had views and ideas on the great international issues of the day, but they were the views of a private man. Now the private man should disappear and the international public servant take his place.

He spoke quietly, with none of the gestures, the raising of the voice over certain phrases, and the waiting for applause that one has come to expect in political speeches. Through newspaper inquiries it had been learned that he was fond of mountain climbing. That was true, he said, although he had never climbed any famous peaks.

"However, that much I know of this sport—that the qualities it requires are just those which I feel we all need today: perseverance and patience, a firm grip on realities, careful but imaginative planning, a clear awareness of the dangers but also of the fact that fate is what we make it and that the safest climber is he who never questions his ability to overcome all difficulties."

The following day, in the vast Assembly Hall, he took the oath of office. The emblem of the United Nations decorated the wall behind him, and from the skylight in the domed ceiling, a single shaft of daylight shone down into the room. Delegates from sixty nations sat facing him in rows of blue upholstered chairs at green leather-topped desks of bleached wood. Behind them were members of the staff, newsmen and visitors.

Trygve Lie introduced Hammarskjöld to the officers of the Assembly, then escorted him to the chair that had lately been his, behind the green marble desk raised high on the podium. Hammerskjöld sat down briefly, and, after Lie had walked off the platform to sit in the section reserved for visitors, he stepped down to the speaker's rostrum to give his inaugural address.

Both Lie and Hammarskjöld were Scandinavians, but there the similarity ended. Lie had come up from the ranks of labor and was the true politician, outspoken, very much of a showman, never missing a chance to express an opinion. During the war years he was head of the Norwegian government-in-exile at London and afterward became Foreign Minister of Norway. He was sensitive to criticism and was driven to giving up his post as Secretary-General because of it, but he had enjoyed his role as a public figure; and at press conferences, facing hundreds of newsmen, newsreel cameras, and television turrets, he was in his element.

"Somewhere during the night I had become what is termed as newsworthy, and my callers wanted me to react," Dag Hammarskjöld said soon after his arrival in New York.

It was obvious from the start that his private life would be kept distinct from his public life. He was not prepared for the sudden publicity he met at every move. He tried various methods of holding press conferences, and though he answered questions freely as long as they touched on his work as Secretary-General, he was never to become accustomed to it. As for the official tasks before him, he was well prepared in background, experience, and temperament to mediate in demands and quarrels, soothe ruffled tempers and keep his own under control, endure criticism and diplomatic coldness when his judgment was impartial.

Three weeks after he took over his duties, he arranged a farewell meeting with Lie and the staff he had organized during his seven years in office.

"Before I leave I shall do one thing I've wanted to do for a long time," Lie announced. "I am going to take all the troubles of the past, all the disappointments, all the headaches, and pack them in a bag and throw them into the East River. I shall carry away with me the memory of all the good things, all the happy things which have made this job one of the most satisfying experiences of my life."

Hammarskjöld settled down to the work before him. He became acquainted with the members of his staff and learned which of them could be relied upon for sound judgment.

"I have come here to be at the service of you all," he said. "I wish to set about all problems without preconceived opinions. It will be your job to judge how I shall succeed in this. It is your job to set me right if I am not succeeding."

The under-secretaries had to be chosen so that all parts of the world would be represented, but that did not mean to Hammarskjöld that they were to represent only their one region. He was always to stress the importance of international responsibility.

"Your life is without a foundation if, in any matter, you choose on your own behalf," he wrote that year in his journal.

He met with the under-secretaries on Friday mornings. There was an air of formality in those meetings, with the protocol of seating arrangements. All were of equal rank and, as in the General Assembly, they were seated alphabetically according to their country. There were a few among them that Hammarskjöld found he could work with best; and with these, there were often informal meetings over luncheon, perhaps, or in the late evenings, as in Stockholm and Paris. Per Lind, who had come with him from Sweden, was one of the group. Another was Heinz Wieschhoff, an anthropologist who had fled from Germany when Hitler came to power. He had spent some time in Africa and was an expert on African affairs. Ahmed Bokhari of Pakistan became a close friend and advisor on Asia. Two Americans he enjoyed working with were Ralph Bunche, who had won the Nobel Peace Prize three years before, and Andrew Cordier, a political scientist from Indiana. Cordier, witty, cheerful, had been with the United Nations since its beginning, and he became one of the most loyal and devoted of Hammarskjöld's friends.

One of the first things the new Secretary-General did was to forbid FBI investigations in search of American Communists in the United Nations. He flatly refused to allow innocent members to be questioned or accused by any nation. If there were any among them who put political interests before his responsibility as an international public servant, it was a matter for the United Nations to take up, he felt.

By July the way had been made clear for a cease-fire agreement in Korea. Stalin's death had affected the Communists in China and North Korea as well as Russia, and they eased their demands for repatriation of war prisoners against their will. A complicated system of inspection by neutral nations was set up to make sure no prisoner was forced to stay or leave. The truce was a hostile one, still armed and suspicious, without victory on either side. Though there was no open warfare anywhere in the world, this still did not mean there was peace, Dag Hammarskjöld warned.

Eleven American airmen, shot down while flying over North Korea, were being held in Peking against the terms of the truce. Trouble was brewing in Indochina, Palestine, Kashmir. There was a Mau Mau uprising in Africa, an H-bomb explosion in Russia, a new nationalism in Egypt with the rise of Nasser to power. Hundreds of thousands of Arabs were made homeless by a change of boundary lines. There had been a time when a local crisis could occur without causing a stir in the rest of the world, but with television, radio, cabled news reports for the daily papers—all these problems were brought quickly and fully into every home. Some called the Secretary-General the President of the world.

As he searched for solutions to each problem as it came up, Hammarskjöld spoke of himself as the servant of seventy-six nations representing the most varied political philosophies and outlooks. "The humility which comes with others having faith in you," he wrote. "If only I may grow: firmer, simpler—quieter, warmer."

In October, 1953, six months after Dag Hammarskjöld had become Secretary-General, his father died at the age of ninety-one. On the desk in his study there was a book of ancient Greek poems he had lately been reading. His chair was turned outward, facing the Humblegarden. The trees were in their autumn foliage, and the jackdaws he had once called messengers from the fields and spires of Uppsala were swarming and bickering about their roosting places as they had been doing year after year.

"Behold, thou hast made my days as it were a span long, and mine age is even in respect to thee—"

Hjalmar Hammarskjöld was buried beside his wife in Uppsala, in the shadows of the tall elms. The year had brought death to him and a new kind of life for his son.

" '—Soon comes the night—.' " As the year ended, Dag Hammarskjöld's thoughts again went back—to the past at Uppsala and to the procession of years since and the ones yet to come. "Let me finish what I have been permitted to begin. Let me give all without any assurance of increase."

Each morning he faced mounds of papers on his desk —some trivial and some so highly important they could change the course of world history. Every one had to be studied, altered perhaps, approved or disapproved, and signed, but the desk was clear by eight o'clock when he closed his office for the night. He was in demand as a public speaker, and there were the United Nations meetings to attend in Paris or Geneva. The keynote of all his speeches was a plea for averting war through negotiations. War in the twentieth century means total war, he warned, fought not only by mass armies but by the entire civilian population. The technique of warfare had been so revolutionized from the First World War, through the Second, and into the hydrogen bomb era that it could bring vast destruction to vast areas and death to millions upon millions of civilians.

A boy of sixteen asked him in a television interview why there was no mention of God in the United Nations Charter. Hammarskjöld explained that in the Preamble of the Charter the nations expressed their faith in the dignity and worth of the human person, and they pledged themselves to practice tolerance and live together in peace with one another as good neighbors. Whatever creed and form of worship—and there were many represented by the member nations—all, he said, could recognize that it was the will of God that we should love our neighbors as ourselves. In the last stanza of one of his poems which no one had ever seen, he wrote:

> Give me a pure heart—that I may see Thee,
> A humble heart—that I may hear Thee,
> A heart of love—that I may serve Thee,
> A heart of faith—that I may abide in Thee.

At another time he compared himself to a pilot guiding a ship through high seas:

> With all the powers of your body concentrated in
>   the hand on the tiller,
> All the powers of your mind concentrated on the
>   goal beyond the horizon,
> You laugh as the salt spray catches your face in
>   the second of rest
> Before a new wave—

Sharing the happy freedom of the moment with those
who share your responsibility.

Beneath the poem he added a thanks to those who had
taught him this and thanks to the days which had taught
him this.

A change of mood came over him after he had settled
down to the responsibilities of his new work. He was like
one who had found the right way after wandering alone
and lost. To his former chief, Finance Minister Wigforss,
he wrote that he was now a perfectly happy man, yet he
felt that now, more than ever, he must be on guard
against the temptations of pride and self-interest that
come to men of high position. "Not I, but God in me," he
reminded himself time and again. "—to be in the hands
of God. Once again a reminder that this is all that
remains for you to live for—and once more the feeling
of disappointment which shows how slow you are to
learn."

Hammarskjöld's first great test as Secretary-General
of the United Nations came at the end of 1954. The
eleven American airmen held captive in Peking since
they had been shot down over North Korea in January
of the year before, had been tried and sentenced as spies.
The United States brought the matter up before the
General Assembly. There the sixteen nations which had
furnished troops for the Korean War drew up a resolution condemning the trial and sentence, and they asked
the Secretary-General to try and obtain the release of
the men by any means he judged appropriate.

Uppsala Castle, 1926. From left: brother Åke, father Hjalmar, brother Sten, mother Agnes, and Dag.

Hammarskjöld brothers. From left: Bo, Dag, Åke, and Sten.

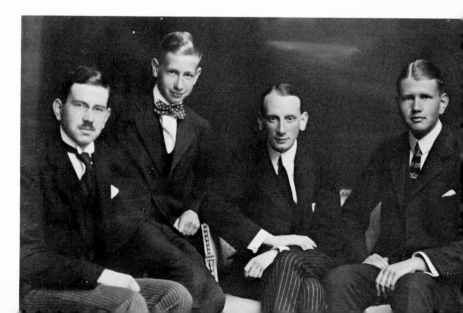

Backåkra. Dag Hammarskjöld located his permanent Swedish home, Backåkra, in the province of Skåne. The farmhouse is built in the traditional Skåne style with an open courtyard. He furnished Backåkra with mementos from around the world. He never lived to see his retreat finished. The home is owned by the Swedish Touring Club and is open to the public part of the year.

Hammarskjöld was in doubt as to what effect the resolution would have. "You either condemn or you negotiate," he said. "You can't do both." And when one of the nations had been denied membership in the Organization, what would be the good of condemning?

A half hour after receiving the request to try and obtain the release of the men, he sent a cable to Chou Enlai, China's Prime Minister, saying he would like to take up the matter with him personally. The reply was not long in coming. The Prime Minister was prepared to receive him in the interest of peace and relaxation of international tension, and to discuss pertinent questions with him. A second cable followed immediately, in true Oriental fashion, declaring that since the conviction of the spies by a Chinese court was a domestic affair, there was no justification for the United Nations trying to interfere.

In spite of the vagueness of the second message, Dag Hammarskjöld went on with his plans for meeting with China's Prime Minister. He was reminded of some lines from the Psalms and wrote them down before leaving:

"*God spake once*, and twice I have also heard the same: that power belongeth unto God:
and that thou, Lord, art merciful: for thou rewardest every man to his work." (*Psalm* 62:11, 12)

The first stop of the journey was Stockholm. After his father's death, Hammarskjöld had been elected to take his place in the Swedish Royal Academy. Now he was present for the inauguration ceremony. The eighteen members of the Academy are elected for life, and only at the death of one member can a new one be chosen. In all its two hundred years of existence, this was the first time a son had succeeded his father to membership. According to tradition, the new member, in his inaugural address, tells about the life and accomplishments of his predecessor. Dressed in formal attire, Dag Hammarskjöld stood before the Royal Family, heads of the government and the seventeen members of the Academy, and spoke about his father. He was objective, speaking not as a son about his father but as one man summing up the life work of another. Yet through it all, the listener caught an undertone of tenderness and admiration.

Both the British and the French prime ministers, who had had conferences with Chou En-lai, warned Hammarskjöld that he'd find Chou a hard man to deal with. There were few negotiators his equal in the world, they said. While in Stockholm, Hammarskjöld made arrangements with his friend Uno Willers, director of the Royal Library, to meet the Chinese ambassador. Willers invited both men to lunch at his home. There they discussed details of the visit, the best route to take, and which of his aides would accompany him. A third meeting had to be held at the home of Willers' mother, for by then the newsmen were on their trail and gave them no peace.

"To have faith—not to hesitate!" Dag Hammarskjöld wrote in his journal on Christmas Day, and five days later, as he was making preparations to leave for China, he again quoted from one of the Psalms: "If I take the wings of the morning and remain in the uttermost parts of the sea; even there thy hand shall lead me." (*Psalm* 139:8)

At the beginning of the year he was reminded of a different hymn familiar to him in his childhood:

> "Nought is given 'neath the sun,
> Nought is had that is not won."
> — (Swedish hymn)

It was bitter cold when Dag Hammarskjöld and his party of five arrived in Peking. Though accustomed to Swedish winters, he was bundled in a fur-collared overcoat and wore a soft felt hat. He and his aides were received with Oriental politeness and hospitality. Dr. Bokhari of Pakistan had come along as his political advisor and expert on Asian affairs. And there was Bill Ranallo, an American of Italian parentage, who was assigned to him as personal aide and bodyguard, to be with him at all times wherever he went.

The first meeting with Chou En-lai was on the sixth of January in the ornate Hall of Western Flowers. Both were men of learning and from aristocratic families with generations of men serving their governments. The Chinese, who had been a student of Western culture in his youth, soon learned that his Scandinavian guest knew as much about Oriental history, poetry, and art.

For thirteen and a half hours, over a period of four afternoons, there were formal discussions between Hammarskjöld and Chou. With a passive face, each was skillful at concealing his inmost thoughts. Hammarskjöld used the same subtle approach as his host, talking around a subject, perhaps discussing a painting of thirteen centuries ago or a poem by Mao Tse-tung, the present Chinese leader, and at the same time conveying the meaning of his mission. He let it be understood that, while the trial and sentencing of Americans shot down over Korea could be considered an internal affair, if there were international repercussions, that was the affair of the United Nations. The People's Republic of China recognized the United Nations Charter, Chou En-lai implied. No promise was made, but there was something in the manner of the prime minister that led Hammarskjöld to believe the airmen would be released. It would have to come as Chou's own decision and not as if pressure had been brought to bear. For that reason, he gave out only the vaguest of press releases after each visit. The talks were useful; relaxation of world tensions had been touched upon. Nothing more was known about the talks of these two men.

Hammarskjöld was fascinated by this ancient country. He and his group were taken on sight-seeing tours, with the chief of protocol as their guide. Each slim, towering pagoda and each yellow roof with vermilion-lacquered walls told something of China's long, continuing history. They saw the splendid Painted Gallery at the Summer Palace, the gilded Hall of Supreme Harmony, the Gate of Heavenly Peace, and the magnificent dome over the Temple of Heaven. They also saw a kind of poverty that was not known in the Swedish welfare state—people in rags, hungry, cold, knowing nothing but the struggle to keep barely alive. A banquet was given for Hammarskjöld and his aides in the Hall of Purple Light on his last evening in China. There were twenty different kinds of food served, including consomme of swallow's nest, shark's fin, and crab meat, sweet potato balls, and cherries with laurel-perfumed syrup.

Over thirteen centuries ago the poet Tu Fu had written:

> Behind the red lacquered gates,
> wine is left to sour, meat to rot.
> Outside the gates lie the bones
> of the frozen and the starved.
> The flourishing and the withered are
> just a foot apart.
> It tears my heart to ponder on it.

"My trip to China was a fantastic experience, and it has left me in a way maturer than before," Dag Hammarskjöld wrote to Bo Beskow in Sweden. "It was magnificent, harrowing, infinitely remote and yet infinitely real. This can be said of both the country (that splendid camp for nomad princes come out of the desert across the narrow mountain range—a camp with an endlessly repeated rhythm of pavilion roofs) and Chou En-lai himself (with a brain of steel, blood on his hands, stern self-discipline, and a very cordial smile)."

Back in New York, Dag Hammarskjöld dared not say anything that would risk the success of his mission.

"The door has been opened and can be kept open, given restraint on both sides," he said at a crowded press conference. The problem was in persuading the Americans to have patience, and do nothing that would prevent a peaceful settlement of the affair. It seemed to him that everybody was afraid of everybody.

By April, with still no word about the release of the captured airmen, the Americans were growing even more restless. Hammarskjöld made a brief visit to Stockholm where he had another meeting with the Chinese ambassador. Again there was an enigmatic statement, no definite promise, nothing to put a finger on, but Hammarskjöld felt sure Chou En-lai would act favorably.

Shortly after this, Uno Willers attended a party at the Soviet Embassy, where he met one of the Chinese diplomats who inquired after his friend, Mr. Hammarskjöld. Willers answered that the Secretary-General would be in Sweden during the summer for his fiftieth birthday. That was interesting, the Chinese said, and he asked what Mr. Hammarskjöld would like for his birthday. Willers might have named many things—a Chinese painting, a silk screen, sculpture, lacquer ware. "But I think he'd like most of all the release of the airmen," he added.

Often in his speeches Hammarskjöld brought in some literary reference, a quotation from a modern French poet or an ancient Chinese sage, or a passage from the sacred books of India. He spoke once of a Swedish poet

now dead who had searched half around the world for a
place he could call the most beautiful. But so beautiful
were they all that none excelled the others. In another
poem he had written: ". . . I yearn for the ground./ I
yearn for the stones where as a child I played."

The same could be said of Dag Hammarskjöld. He had
traveled around the world and had seen the beauty of
every place. But something in him would always yearn
for his native land. For the two years he had been in
New York, home to him was an eight-room apartment on
Park Avenue in the Seventies. It had been chosen for him
before his arrival, but, by the time he had finished with
the decoration, it was a constant reminder of Sweden.
The bookshelves were filled from top to bottom, but the
walls of the living and dining rooms were white and
almost bare with the exception of a few modern Swedish
paintings. The furniture, modern with simple lines, was
made in Scandinavia, as were the rugs and draperies.
Over the fireplace hung a climber's alpenstock given to
him by the Sherpa guide, Tensing, who, with Edmund
Hillary, had been the first to climb Mount Everest. In
the same spring Hammarskjöld had become Secretary-
General, they had planted the United Nations flag with
the flags of their own countries at the summit. Carved on
the alpenstock was the inscription: "So that you may
climb on to greater heights."

In 1955 Hammarskjöld became the owner of a country home in Sweden. It was a typical farmhouse in the
Skåne province, a hundred and fifty years old, with a
thatched roof, sturdy old beams and batten doors. It was

built around a courtyard and overlooking the sea and the moors, a place where he could get away from the cares of his office. The place was found for him by Bo Beskow who, now married to a quiet, attractive young woman, owned the land adjoining.

The United Nations held a commemoration of its tenth birthday in June of that year. Dag Hammarskjöld went to San Francisco for the ceremonies. On his way he stopped at Baltimore to deliver the commencement address at Johns Hopkins University. He also spoke at Stanford and the University of California at Berkeley. In August he was to be in Geneva for the opening of the International Scientific Conference on the peaceful uses of atomic energy and international cooperation in developing this energy. But in July there would be a few weeks free to spend in his new home. After he had drawn up his annual report to present to the next session of the General Assembly, Hammarskjöld, with his personal aide, Bill Ranallo, took a plane for Sweden.

In Stockholm, Uno Willers told of two telephone calls that had come from the Chinese Embassy in recent weeks, checking on the date of Dag Hammarskjöld's birthday. It was obvious that something was being planned. Days of suspense followed, but July 29 came and went, and nothing happened. "Thomas Aquinas: Why do you seek rest? You were only created to labor," Hammarskjöld wrote on his fiftieth birthday.

Even in this quiet spot between the sea and the moors, there was no peace from the crowds of newsmen and photographers that followed wherever he went. On the first of August, three days later, Bo Beskow and his wife took Hammarskjöld out on the water in a small fishing boat to get away from the crowds. When they returned at the end of the day, they found what seemed to be the whole population of Skåne waiting for them, waving little flags in greeting. The message had arrived from China. The eleven American airmen would be released.

Dag Hammarskjöld would take no credit for this event. Many different things had happened to bring this about, he said, and many people were involved. But he added that no event or anything which he had been permitted to do ranked higher on that list of causes for gratitude than his trip to Peking.

He wrote that night to a friend, "Today we accomplished something, God and I. That is to say it was God who built while I stood below with the paintpot, shouting."

And to himself he wrote, as a warning against pride: "Shame mixed with gratitude; shame over all my bouts of vanity, envy, and self-complacency—gratitude for all to which my bare intention, though certainly not my achievement, may possibly have entitled me. God sometimes allows us to take the credit—for His work. Or withdraws from it in His solitude. He watches our capers on the stage with an ironic smile—so long as we do not tamper with the scales of justice."

Again he remembered the Psalms and referred to them in his journal as he so often did at times of strong emotion. The first two words of a verse "God spake. . . ." reminded him that power belonged to God. And he added: "And, a few verses earlier: 'As for the children of men, they are but vanity. The children of men are deceitful upon the weights. Give not yourselves unto vanity.' (*Psalm* 62:9, 10) 'Not unto us, O Lord, but unto thy Name give the praise . . .' (*Psalm* 115:1)"

SIX

1955–1956

"This is one of the most important events in the post-war world," Dag Hammarskjöld said of the Atoms for Peace Conference held in Geneva on the eighth of August, 1955. When the plan was first proposed at the General Assembly the year before, it had met an enthusiastic response from all the members. Seventy-three member nations, including the Soviet bloc, offered to send their leading scientists and share the secrets of their discoveries. This could be the first step toward cooperation and mutual trust among nations.

The world's leading nuclear scientists were called upon to act as an advisory committee for the Secretary-General. Hammarskjöld, though not a scientist, impressed the men with his grasp of the issues under discussion. If a political argument threatened, he steered the subject back to neutral grounds. An American scientist said of him, "He was patient and fair. He listened to both sides. When he made a decision, he expressed it in such a way we accepted it as an end of the matter and it left no bad feelings."

The scientists were concerned with the search for truth and with the idea of brotherhood based on the belief that all knowledge is universal, Hammarskjöld declared at the opening of the meeting. He spoke of the feeling of guilt which has universally been felt, that man in his folly should have thought of no better use of a great discovery than to manufacture with its help the deadliest instruments of annihilation. The scientists could, with an exchange of scientific data, inspire confidence, and the trend of their discussions could turn men's thoughts from war to peace.

An exhibition was arranged under an enormous tent to show how atomic energy could be used for peaceful purposes. To the people looking on, this strange discovery was still something so mysterious, so much to be dreaded, that their minds went back to the time, ten years ago that month, when the first atomic bomb fell on Hiroshima. Now they saw that this same power could be used in man's fight against sickness, hunger, cold, poverty. It could supply fuel and the power to run ships, planes, and tractors. With its use, ocean water could be desalted, and deserts could be turned into fertile green fields.

A few weeks before, in this same city, the heads of the United States, Russia, Great Britain, and France had held their summit meeting. Since Stalin's death, Russia had had a collective leadership meeting. Prime Minister Bulganin was accompanied by one unknown outside the country until just recently—Nikita Khrushchev who was just emerging as a contender for supreme power. There had been a spirit of good will and optimism at that meeting of world leaders, as there was at the Atoms for Peace Conference, with promises of no aggressive wars and a vague hope of sharing military as well as scientific knowledge.

Before the summer was over, trouble had flared up in the Middle East. In that ancient land where civilization had its beginning, five proud nations had been given their independence since the end of World War II. Egypt, Syria, Jordan, and Lebanon had been under foreign rule for over five hundred years, first as part of the Turkish Empire and later under British or French mandate. And the people of Israel had been homeless since the time of the Roman Empire. In 1947, the United Nations had partitioned an irregular area of 8000 square miles for them, with boundaries touching all four Arab countries. Hundreds of thousands of Arabs, whose home this had been for countless centuries, were forced to leave, and now they were the homeless ones. From the beginning there had been hostility, both religious and political, with border raids and border fights. A truce had been drawn up by the United Nations in 1948, only to be broken again and again.

"History has placed a burden on our shoulders," Dag Hammarskjöld had said in a speech before leaving for Geneva. He had compared these nations, so long dependent on others and now emerging as strong, dynamic national states, to a young man coming of age—conscious of his powers, eager to find his own way, to make his voice heard, and to offer his contribution to progress. But the creative urges of these nations were tinged with strong emotions of the past.

"It is for all of us, denying neither the good nor the ills of that past, to look ahead and not to permit old conflicts to envenom the spirit of the creative work before us," he had said.

At the end of August, Israel complained to the Security Council of attacks by Egyptian soldiers at the border of the Negev desert. A week later Egypt complained that the Israelis had killed thirty-six Egyptian soldiers and refugees in Gaza. The United Nations Truce Supervisory Organization had an able commander in charge and, working through him, Hammarskjöld brought a stop to the border raids and retaliations. But it was only a temporary measure in this land that had been fought over for thousands of years and where memories of old conflicts and old hatreds would not die.

On Christmas Eve he wrote: " 'O God, thou art my God . . . in a barren and dry land where no water is. Thus have I looked for thee in the sanctuary, that I might behold thy power and glory.' (*Psalm* 63:1–3) "

In January, 1956, Hammarskjöld went on a mission to Asia and Australia. On his way he stopped off at the Middle East to meet and talk with the heads of the Egyptian and Israeli governments. Three years before, Egypt had thrown out an incompetent king and his corrupt government, and a republic was proclaimed.

Gamal Abdel Nasser, one of the group of army officers that brought on the revolt, was now the country's prime minister and the real ruler. He came from a middle-class provincial family, the son of a post-office civil servant. Though he accepted aid for his country from both Russia and the United States, he was interested neither in Communism nor the Western type of democracy. His concern then was for land reform in Egypt, for the confiscating of land from the wealthy landowners and distributing it to the peasants. He was a soldier and inexperienced at that time in governing. Hammarskjöld, in his talks with Nasser, sensed that he was insecure and that the West did not understand him as it should. The Egyptian Foreign Minister, Dr. Mahmoud Fawzi, a diplomat, scholar, and an aristocrat who had been in government service for a long time, was one Hammarskjöld could feel closer to. Both Egyptians had a long list of grievances against Israel, putting the blame on that country for the conflict.

Hammarskjöld left Egypt and went on to Israel, where he met David Ben-Gurion, who had come back from retirement to become prime minister for a second time. Dynamic, intensely patriotic, mixing political pronouncements with quotations from the Old Testament, Ben-Gurion was likened to some patriarch of old. Hammarskjöld was fascinated by his personality. Once, on a visit to Burma, Ben-Gurion had shocked the more orthodox among the Israelis by taking instruction in the philosophy of Buddhism. To set an example of pioneering to the youth of his country, he made his home at

Sdeh Boker, a settlement on the Negev desert, in a land
he would have no longer barren and dry where no water
was. The two men had a respect and admiration for each
other, and would probably have enjoyed quiet discussions on Buddhism if there had not been the urgent
problem before them. Also Ben-Gurion could not forgive
Hammarskjöld for negotiating with Nasser. If one was
not prejudiced in his favor, then he must be prejudiced
against him, he believed.

"We'll give two blows for one!" Ben-Gurion had proclaimed when the Egyptians attacked at the border.

Hammarskjöld tried to persuade him to take the
matter up with the United Nations instead of counter-
attacking. The UN hadn't been able to do anything
about it so far, Ben-Gurion replied. He had acted as any
other head of state would have done. He reminded Hammarskjöld that his small country was surrounded by
four unfriendly Arab states, armed and waiting to attack. The old law of an eye for an eye and a tooth for a
tooth still held.

Arab refugees on the Jordan border made raids against
Israel. Israeli troops struck back, killing fifty in one
night. Thirty-two Egyptian soldiers paid with their
lives when bridges, roads, and water-pipe lines were
blown up in Egypt. Syrian Arabs opened fire on fishing
boats on the Sea of Galilee, and Israel's soldiers swept
across the border in retaliation. More and more raids and
forays occurred until they were becoming almost a
daily event.

On his return from Asia and Australia, Dag Hammar-

skjöld had the matter brought up before the Security
Council. His visit to the Middle East in January had
been on his own and was not a United Nations assign-
ment. He felt that by trying the same quiet diplomacy
he had used in China to bring about the release of the
airmen, he would accomplish more than an open debate.
At the request of the Security Council, which had voted
unanimously, Hammarskjöld, with his chosen aides, returned to the Middle East. He established headquarters
at Beirut, Lebanon, and from there visited the five belligerent countries and talked with their leaders.

From Syria and Lebanon there were complaints that
the waters of the Jordan River, which flowed also
through their land, was being tapped and diverted near
its source. In Israel Hammarskjöld again talked with Ben-
Gurion over endless pots of tea, trying to bring him to
an agreement on a cease-fire order. While he was there,
he was taken to a couple of collective farm settlements.
Where there had formerly been a few scattered mud
huts of the Arabs, he saw neat red-roofed farmhouses
built in a circle around a group of community buildings.
Behind each house, in widening strips of land shaped like
slices of pie, there were sleek cows or sheep, leghorn
chickens, olive groves, vineyards, orchards, and fields of
vegetables and grain.

He had seen such experiments in India a few months
earlier. There he had found the same kind of courage and
enthusiasm. The land in India was rich, but the people
there were devoting all their energies to taking the giant
step from the primitive agricultural systems of their

country to the methods of a modern industrial society, he said. But here were people who had stepped out of the highly organized and specialized industrial life of the West and were pioneering in building up a strong economy on a barren soil. They had come from all parts of the world—from Poland, Turkey, the United States, Czechoslovakia, and from Hungary, Austria, Italy, and Germany. Some bore the marks of concentration camps. Now the horrors of persecution, of torture and death chambers, were in the past. Back in the land which had been promised to Abraham and to all his seed, where Isaac had built cisterns and prospered, where Jacob had wrestled with the angel, and where Moses had led the Israelites out from bondage in Egypt, they were turning a scorched desert into green hills and fertile valleys.

Hammarskjöld took time out from his official duties in Israel to call on Martin Buber, a great religious philosopher whose works he had long admired. Buber had had the courage to stand up against Prime Minister Ben-Gurion and protest that the Arab minority in Israel were being treated as second-rate citizens.

In Gaza Dag Hammarskjöld had seen some of the 900,000 Arab refugees who had been driven off this land that had been theirs for two thousand years. They, too, claimed Abraham, to whom the land had been promised, as their ancestor. The neighboring Arab countries would not take them in, insisting that they should be returned to Israel. And in Israel there was no room for them.

"The suffering of the refugee children is particularly shocking from a humanitarian point of view," Hammarskjöld wrote later for the UN Save-the-Children Fund. "Many of these children were born into a refugee existence and have no experience of any other way of life. Social security, civic rights and duties, all the things that we others regard as self-evident elements of life, if it is to be worth living, are concepts unknown to many of them. As they grow up, they come to realize that their existence is not a normal one, and find that they cannot be fully valid members of society until they have ceased to be refugees. It is the duty of those of us who are more fortunately placed to help them achieve this."

On May 9, after his return to New York, Hammarskjöld was able to report to the Security Council that he had written agreements from Egypt, Israel, Jordan, Syria, and Lebanon that the cease-fire would be observed. This was only a first step, but it was an important one.

With an end to border violence, the United Nations could get on with important decisions which he said had been too long neglected. There were the Arab refugees, hundreds of thousands of them, a problem very much on everybody's mind in the region, and until these people were resettled and repatriated, there could be no real peace in the Middle East; an agreement must be reached on water rights to the rivers flowing through boundary lines; demilitarized zones must be disarmed. There were debates in the Security Council where these grievances were aired and, in July, Hammarskjöld was again in the Middle East for negotiations.

While he was in the midst of conferences in Israel,

word came that the United States had withdrawn its offer of a loan to Egypt for construction of the High Aswan Dam. Nasser, in retaliation, nationalized the Suez Canal, closed it to Israeli ships, and announced that profits from the Canal would be used to build the dam at Aswan. Britain and France, principal stockholders with Egypt, began military preparations immediately. Warships were sent to the Mediterranean, and troops were stationed on the Island of Cyprus, alert for an attack. Border incidents flared up again and the cease-fire agreement came to an end. Russia stepped in with offers of military help to Egypt.

This meant for the Secretary-General going back to start all over again. He expressed his thoughts in his journal at that time by several quotations from the writings of philosophy and from the Psalms:

" 'I believe verily to see the goodness of the Lord in the land of the living.

O tarry thou the Lord's leisure: be strong and he shall comfort thine heart.' (*Psalm* 27 :15, 16) "

A month later, at the end of one of his many trying days of that summer, he wrote another reminder to himself:

"It is an *idea* you are serving—an idea which must be victorious if a mankind worth the name is to survive. It is this idea which you must help towards victory with all your strength. . . . Knowing this, it should be easy for you to smile at criticism of decisions misunderstood,

ridicule of expressions misinterpreted as 'idealism,' dec-
larations of war to the death upon that which, for all outward appearances, you are devoting your life. But is
it so easy? No—for the pettiness you show in your reactions to other people about whose motives *you* know
nothing, renders you—very justly—vulnerable to the
pettiness you encounter in the interpretations of your
own efforts."

He thought of his country home in Sweden and the
few peaceful summer months he had planned to spend
there but could not. In September he wrote nostalgically
to Bo Beskow: "The world is a bit mad, and the more one
is compelled to have to do with it, the more one longs for
good, wise friends in some quiet corner where you don't
listen to radio, and are interested in the migrant birds
that now, I suppose, have passed over Rytterskulle and
gone back to the Nile and its frogs."

It was about that time that a plan began to take shape
in his mind for a room to be set aside in the United
Nations building for quiet meditation.

Britain and France decided to take the matter of the
Suez Canal before the Security Council. The first meeting took place on October 5. Since Egypt was not a
member of the Council, Dr. Fawzi had been asked to be
there to represent his country. The foreign ministers of
Britain, France, and Russia, and Secretary Dulles of the
United States also attended. The debates were orderly
and well presented, but nothing was accomplished. Hammarskjöld then turned to private discussions, with the

foreign ministers of Britain, France, and Egypt gathered around a low coffee table with him in his office on the thirty-eighth floor to talk informally. When one rejected a proposal, he was asked to suggest an alternative that would be agreeable to all. French Foreign Minister Pineau said later that Dag Hammarskjöld did not propose solutions. Instead, he noted the points where he could see the possibility of an agreement.

Within a week an agreement was reached on six general principles, including one that the operation was to be kept out of the politics of any country. The Security Council voted to accept this agreement. Hammarskjöld had further talks with Foreign Secretary Fawzi to prepare the way to a solution to the problems of international control of the Canal and freedom of navigation to the ships of all nations.

"A very great crisis is behind us," President Eisenhower announced in a speech on television.

This optimism was suddenly crushed when, on October 29, Israel announced that 32,000 of its troops had crossed the border into Sinai to wipe out the bases of the Egyptian raiders. The United States called for an emergency meeting of the Security Council. A resolution was drawn up, calling for the withdrawal of the troops and instructing member nations not to intervene by use of threat or force. After hours of debate, a vote was taken. Russia joined the United States in approving the resolution, but it was vetoed by France and Britain.

It was near midnight when Hammarskjöld returned to his apartment. He was deeply depressed, for he felt betrayed by the very ones whose integrity he had most relied upon. That very afternoon an ultimatum had been issued from London and read before the Council: unless both Egyptian and Israeli forces had withdrawn within twelve hours to a distance of ten miles from the Canal, British and French forces would intervene. Their naval units, already stationed in the Mediterranean, had begun steaming toward the Suez and Israel's army was advancing steadily across the Sinai Peninsula to join them.

Sleep would not come to Dag Hammarskjöld that night. His Swedish housekeeper Nellie found him still at his desk at dawn, working on his speech in longhand. The Council met again that afternoon, the last day of October. Dag Hammarskjöld stood beside his chair at the center of the huge horseshoe-shaped table. On the wall behind him there was a mural representing man's efforts to emerge from a dark past of war and bondage to a life of peace and freedom.

"The principles of the charter are, by far, greater than the Organization in which they are embodied, and the aims which they are to safeguard are holier than the policies of any single nation or people." He spoke calmly, but something in his voice, the pitch, a more pronounced accent, betrayed his emotion. He went on:

"As a servant of the organization, the Secretary-General has the duty to maintain his usefulness by avoiding public stands on conflicts between member nations unless and until such an action might help to resolve the conflict. He must also be a servant of the principles of the Charter, and its aim must ultimately determine for him what is right and wrong. For that he must stand. A Secretary-General cannot serve on any other assumption than that—within the necessary limits of human frailty and honest differences of opinion—all member nations honor their pledge to observe all the articles of the Charter. He should also be able to assume that those organs which are charged with the task of upholding the Charter will be in a position to fulfill their task.

"The bearing of what I have just said must be obvious to all without any elaboration from my side. Were the members to consider that another view of the duties of the Secretary-General than the one here stated would better serve the organization, it is their obvious right to act accordingly."

This was taken as an offer to resign if that was the wish of the members of the Council. Immediately there were expressions of confidence by the representatives of all the member nations, and an acceptance of the right of the Secretary-General to act according to the principles of the Charter.

Henry Cabot Lodge, speaking for the United States said, "We share the opinions just expressed and the concept of his duties." The Soviet representative spoke of his confidence in the Secretary-General. The French and British representatives also mentioned their high regard for his integrity and impartiality.

The Security Council was powerless to act when two of the permanent members vetoed the cease-fire proposal. The matter would have to be taken up before the General Assembly and acted upon by all the seventy-six member nations. An emergency meeting was called for the following day at four in the afternoon.

Sometime during that morning Dag Hammarskjöld wrote in his journal more lines from the Psalms as an expression of his thoughts and prayers: " 'I will lay me down in peace, and take my rest: for it is thou, Lord, only, that makest me dwell in safety.' (*Psalm* 4:9)" And " 'Hold thee still in the Lord . . . fret not thyself, else shalt thou be moved to evid.' (*Psalm* 37:7, 8)"

The day was rainy and dismal, and a winter darkness had set in by four in the afternoon when the meeting opened. The Secretary-General had been in his office since early morning, holding hurried conferences and drawing plans for a possible reconciliation. The atmosphere was tense in the General Assembly Hall on that day. Representatives from all the member nations were there. Both sides were entitled to be heard, and any who wanted had a right to speak and state his position. Through this organization they spoke to the whole world. From the glass-enclosed booths along the side walls, interpreters translated simultaneously; broadcasters and cameramen sent out every word and gesture.

Secretary of State Dulles had flown in from Washington. He proposed a resolution urging a cease-fire at once and steps taken to reopen the Canal. In his speech he paid tribute to Dag Hammarskjöld for his great contribution to the efforts of a just and peaceful solution. He asked that the Secretary-General take on the responsibility of observing and reporting on the matter for any further action by the United Nations.

The debates were long, and the meeting lasted until

four o'clock in the morning, with only a short break in the early evening. None of the nations involved were without blame. England and France, principal stock-holders of that strip of water running through Egyptian territory between the Mediterranean and the Red Sea, gave as the reason for their action the need for protecting the Canal; yet their ships and planes were already bombing Egyptian airfields and military installations in violation of their pledges to the United Nations Charter. Egypt had been wronged, but Egypt was guilty of boycotting Israel and closing the Canal to Israeli ships. Israel had suffered border raids, its citizens been killed and property destroyed, but Israel's troops were engaged in aggressive warfare, occupying the entire Sinai Peninsula in Egypt, with a thousand Egyptians killed and six thousand taken prisoner. The Soviets, now openly allied with Egypt, spoke of the sovereign rights of that country when, only the week before, Hungarian patriots had risen in revolt against Russian rule and put their former prime minister, Imre Nagy, back in power, with a promise of free elections which the Russians had denied them. There was not one among member nations that had not broken the United Nations pledge to renounce force and to settle their disputes by peaceful means, conforming with the principles of justice and international law.

Hammarskjöld listened to speech after speech in silence. No one could read his thoughts, but the lines of worry on his face were evident. He had once remarked that everyone in his own eyes had a good case, and there must be some element in his case that could be recognized as right. At some time that year, in an undated passage of his journal, he wrote:

With the love of Him who knows all,
With the patience of Him Whose now is eternal,
With the righteousness of Him who has never failed,
With the humility of Him who has suffered all the
                    possibilities of betrayal.

A vote was taken the next night, after more hours of debate, on a resolution that had been drawn up in the Secretary-General's office. In addition to a cease-fire order, a United Nations Emergency Force would be organized to keep order while the troops on both sides were being withdrawn. It would be the world's first army with the command, not to fight but to prevent fighting. The Soviet Union switched sides over this and joined Britain and France in opposition, but in the General Assembly each member nation, however small, has an equal vote with the others, and the resolution passed. A request was made to the Secretary-General to have a report ready on the Emergency Force within forty-eight hours.

It was long after midnight when the meeting was adjourned. The weary delegates were on the point of leaving when a message was read, saying that an emergency meeting of the Security Council would be held immediately. The representatives took their places around the curved table of the Council Hall, to remain there for the rest of the night. Reports had been coming in during the night that Soviet troops had begun an attack on Budapest to overthrow the Hungarian People's Republic which had been re-established the week before. Prime Minister Nagy sent an appeal for help to the people of the world, the last word ever to be heard from him again. The capital had been surrounded by a thousand Soviet tanks firing phosphorus shells to burn the city out.

For the next forty-eight hours events were happening that could easily have touched off the spark to another world war. The Soviet Union, with a Communistic government safely restored in Hungary, now turned its attention to the Middle East. An ultimatum was issued, declaring Russia would use force to crush the aggressors and establish peace in that region. The British and French airborne invasion was under way, with troops advancing on Port Said. Israeli soldiers also were steadily advancing.

The Secretary-General worked with almost superhuman energy, getting together the United Nations Emergency Force in the time given him. He called on the smaller neutral nations acceptable to both sides for help. Canada, Colombia, Denmark, Finland, Pakistan, and his own country, Sweden, promised men. Italy offered the use of its airport near Naples as a starting base for the troops, and Switzerland offered to fly them to Egypt on its airlines.

"Aren't you tired?" Leif Belfrage of the Swedish Foreign Office asked during a transatlantic telephone conversation with him.

"No," Hammarskjöld answered. "I don't think I've slept more than two or three hours this past week, but I'm doing fine."

President Eisenhower said of him: "We must avoid in any way interfering with the delicate negotiations now going on under the leadership of Secretary-General Hammarskjöld. We must not do anything that could in any way delay his operations, hinder, or harm them. And I should like to use a moment to speak of what he is doing. He has not only shown his ability. The man has displayed a physical endurance that is highly remarkable, if not unique. Night after night he has made do with one or two hours of sleep, and worked both day and night, and, I might say, worked with intelligence and devotion."

By November 7 the plans for organizing the Emergency Force were completed. Egypt and Israel agreed to a cease-fire, and by midnight Britain and France had ordered their troops to stop fighting.

"We may have been saved from the very edge of a catastrophe," one of the delegates said at the General Assembly.

During this time Dag Hammarskjöld had been keeping an eye on events in Hungary. The prime minister of the new regime issued a statement that the Soviet troops were there at the request of the Hungarian government. Hammarskjöld appointed an investigating committee, but he was informed that the presence of United Nations observers was not justified. He offered to go to Hungary himself, but this was refused also. He would be received as a private citizen only and not in any official capacity, he was told. Without permission from the country involved, the UN was powerless to act.

Egypt, on the other hand, agreed to allow the United Nations troops to enter the country.

"On behalf of the Egyptian armed forces I welcome you as guests, as troops of the United Nations Emergency Force," the Egyptian brigadier general said to the first arrivals of forty-five blue-helmeted men from Denmark and Norway. The next day Dag Hammarskjöld flew in with fifty-four Colombians. He assured Nasser and Fawzi that the troops would remain only long enough to restore peace and to clear the Canal of the sunken ships that now blocked its passage. Within a month, there were 3700 men from eight neutral nations. The British and French began withdrawing their troops. On December 22 the last transport sailed away from Port Said and the Israeli army was pushing back toward its boundary. Peace was restored. Now began the task of clearing the Canal for navigation.

Christmas found Dag Hammarskjöld back in Egypt to spend the holidays with the UN troops on duty there. A Norway spruce had been flown in and decorated, and a special Christmas dinner was prepared for the men, which the Secretary-General, wearing the UN insignia in his buttonhole, shared with them. There was good reason to rejoice that Christmas. Twice it had been proven that war could be averted through the action of the United Nations.

On Christmas Eve Hammarskjöld reminded himself: "Your own efforts 'did not bring it to pass,' only God—

but rejoice if God found a use for your efforts in His work. Rejoice if you feel that what you did was 'necessary,' but remember, even so, that you were simply the instrument by means of which He added one tiny grain to the Universe He has created for His own purposes."

On the day after Christmas he felt again the need of a warning against pride and vanity: "Vanity rears its ridiculous little head and holds up the distorting mirror in front of you. For an instant, the play actor adjusts his smile and his features to the role. For a mere instant— but one too many. It is at such times that you invite defeat and betray Him whom you serve."

SEVEN
1957–1960

"Suez was my third child," Dag Hammarskjöld wrote to Bo Beskow. "Its parents arrived here in a state of great perplexity and some fury. God knows how it will go—but the baby isn't screaming too much now, and perhaps with good help, I shall teach it to walk . . ."

By March, 1957, the last of the Israeli soldiers had returned to their home base, and by the end of April the Suez Canal was cleared of all obstructions and ready for navigation. The Emergency Force, working under American engineers, raised and removed forty-five large objects, including sunken ships, barges, machinery, and a fallen railroad bridge. The Egyptian government agreed to pay the cost of this—over eight million dollars—by placing a levy on the Canal tolls. The French and British stockholders would be paid the full amount of their hold-

ABOVE LEFT, Secretary-General Trygve Lie welcomes his successor as he arrives in New York City from Sweden. ABOVE RIGHT, The new Secretary-General and Professor Ahmed S. Bokhari, taken just after Hammarskjöld was installed April 10, 1953. BELOW, Dag Hammarskjöld takes the oath of office.

TOP, An informal conference between Hammarskjöld and some
high officials of his Executive Office. From left: Leo Malania,
Victor Mills, Andrew W. Cordier, Dag Hammarskjöld, and
Brian E. Urquhart. MIDDLE, The Secretary-General at a meeting
with Prime Minister Chou En-lai of the Chinese People's Republic, in Peking, China, in January of 1955. BELOW LEFT, Dag
Hammarskjöld and Ralph Bunche, Under-Secretary, having an
informal talk while on their way to a meeting. BELOW RIGHT,
On a visit to New Delhi in 1956 Hammarskjöld receives a traditional greeting from two village women at a Community Project
village near New Delhi.

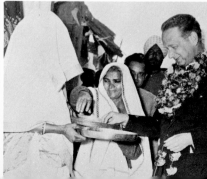

ings, and the right of passage on the Canal would be open to ships of all nations.

A short period of peace followed, which Hammarskjöld compared to a convalescence after an illness, a lull after the sound and the fury. But it was only a lull in a never-ending search for peace. On his return from one of his many trips to the Middle East, he passed the time on the plane by reading an English translation of an ancient book on Chinese history. He came across a passage about the philosopher Sung Tzu and his disciples who had lived some 2200 years ago which struck a familiar note to him.

Constantly rebuffed but never discouraged, they went round from State to State helping people to settle their differences, arguing against wanton attack and pleading for the suppression of arms, that the age in which they lived might be saved from its state of continual war. To this end they interviewed princes and lectured the common people, nowhere meeting with any great success, but obstinately persisting in their task, till kings and commoners alike grew weary of listening to them. Yet undeterred they continued to force themselves on people's attention.

Hammarskjöld smiled at the irony of it, yet there was a touch of pathos about it, and he was reminded of the work of the United Nations constantly trying to save this present age from its state of continual war. He had been with the organization for four years; now his term of office was soon to expire. There was no voice of objection in the Security Council when he was recommended for a second term. The General Assembly passed upon it unanimously. "Let Dag do it" was becoming a slogan. He had brought to the office an importance and responsibility it had not had before. He had taken on more power, but no more than the Charter granted him and no more than was needed for the particular task he faced. The president of the General Assembly spoke of him as the supreme international civil servant, scrupulously objective, self-effacing.

Whether the service of the United Nations bore immediate fruit or not, it was profoundly meaningful, Dag Hammarskjöld said in his acceptance speech of September 26. If it paved one more inch of the road ahead, one was more than rewarded whatever setbacks might follow. If a mountain wall is once climbed, later failures do not undo the fact that it has been shown it *can* be climbed. He ended his speech with these words: "Future generations may come to say of us that we never achieved what we set out to do. May they never be entitled to say that we failed because we lacked faith or permitted narrow self-interest to distort our efforts."

The Meditation Room, remodeled from a seldom-used room off the lobby of the General Assembly, was opened to the public that year. It had been planned, down to the last detail, by Hammarskjöld. Even during the trying times of the Suez crisis, he had taken time to supervise the work. He wanted it utterly simple. There should be nothing to distract the attention, or break upon the inner stillness of those who used the room. "We all have within us a center of stillness surrounded by si-

lence," he wrote for a leaflet to be given to the visitors of
the room.

Except for one large block of iron ore which he had
had sent from Sweden, the room was bare, yet there was
no sense of emptiness about it. The stone he chose because
it was something permanent and firm in a world of
movement and change. It had the weight and solidity of
the everlasting, he said. "We see it as an altar, empty
not because there is no God, not because it is an altar to
an unknown god, but because it is dedicated to the God
whom man worships under many names and in many
forms."

On the wall opposite the entrance door there is a
large abstract painting by Bo Beskow harmonizing in
design and color so softly with the rest of the room that
one is scarcely aware it is there.

It is a room for men of all faiths. A visitor entering
this place of twilight darkness, lit by a single shaft of
light shining down on the rock, meditates and prays in
his own way to his own God. For that reason there are
none of the familiar religious symbols—only the symbols common to all mankind. To Dag Hammarskjöld the
shaft of light was a symbol of how, daily, the light of
the skies gives life to the earth and how the light of the
spirit gives life to matter. He saw in the iron of the rock a
reminder of the necessity for a choice between destruction and construction, between war and peace. Of iron
man has forged his swords; of iron he has also made his
plowshares, he said. Of iron he has constructed tanks, but
of iron he has likewise built his homes: "The block of

iron ore is part of the wealth we have inherited on this earth of ours. How are we to use it?"

At the end of his text in the leaflet, he wrote: "There is an ancient saying that the sense of a vessel is not in its shell but in the void. So it is with this room. It is for those who come here to fill the void with what they find in the center of their stillness."

At about the time of writing this, he also wrote on the pages which he called negotiations with himself—and with God: " 'The Uncarved Block'—remain at the Center, which is yours and that of all humanity. For those goals which it gives to your life, do the utmost which, at each moment, is possible for you. Also, act without thinking of the consequences, or seeking anything for yourself."

The United Nations had become something more than a house for political debate since Dag Hammarskjöld had become Secretary-General four years before. He had a portable stage constructed for the General Assembly Hall so there could be concerts, plays, or ballet performances for the staff to enjoy. He always took part in deciding the program. It became a tradition on United Nations Day for the symphony program to include the final movement of Beethoven's *Ninth Symphony*. The Museum of Modern Art gave him permission to borrow paintings from its collection to hang on the walls of his offices and the private dining room on the 38th floor. He made the selection himself and decided upon how they were hung.

Occasionally he invited musicians, artists, and writers whose works he enjoyed to a small informal luncheon or dinner. It was a welcome change from the formal, protocol-filled dinners he gave for visiting diplomats. St.-John Perse, whose book of poems *Chronique* he was translating into Swedish, was a guest he especially enjoyed. He brought together people who would have interests in common. Pablo Casals, Fritz Kreisler, and Leonard Bernstein, with their wives, were invited to luncheon on a day after Casals had given a concert at the United Nations. John Steinbeck and his wife were his guests, and so was Carl Sandburg whose father had immigrated from Sweden almost a century ago.

The year 1958 came in peacefully. "So shall the world be created each morning anew, *forgiven*—in Thee, by Thee," Dag Hammarskjöld wrote. But before many months passed, trouble started brewing again in the Middle East.

This time it was among the Arab nations. In May, Lebanon, after an attempted revolution, brought a complaint before the Security Council, accusing Nasser's United Arab Republic and the Soviet Union of intervening in its domestic affairs. An observation group was sent to that country by the United Nations under the direction of Secretary-General Hammarskjöld. It arrived in Lebanon about the middle of June, and a week later Hammarskjöld made a quick trip to the capitals of the countries involved. He had scarcely returned to New York when, on July 14, a sudden revolt flared up in Iraq. The king, crown prince, and most of the royal family were assassinated, and a republic was proclaimed —all within twenty-four hours.

Immediately an alarmed Lebanon, and Jordan as

well, sent appeals to Great Britain and the United States for help. Both countries, acting independently of the United Nations, responded by sending troops to the Middle East. Ten thousand American marines landed in Lebanon, and British paratroopers from Cyprus flew into Jordan. The Soviet Union protested over what she called active aggression. There were heated arguments from both sides over the moral issues involved.

To Hammarskjöld, this was a matter that concerned, not the Soviet Union, the United States, or Great Britain, but the Arab nations only. And only they could solve it. Peace could not be imposed by the use of armed forces from the outside, he declared. Once more he trusted to quiet diplomacy. In his private office he talked with foreign ministers and diplomats, consulted with his aides, and then took another trip to the Middle East. It was said of him that he didn't say "Don't do this or don't do that," but he made it clear that there was a better way.

He gave the opening address at the emergency session of the General Assembly on August 8. In it he urged all the nations to work within the United Nations for a peaceful solution. He made an appeal to the Arab States to cooperate with each other and to return to the principles of their earlier agreement of mutual respect for each other's territories, integrity, and sovereignty, and to the agreement of nonaggression and noninterference in each other's internal affairs. His next appeal was to the rest of the world, especially to the Great Powers, to respect and support this movement and allow the Arab people to shape their own destinies in the best interests of each nation within the region and of the region as a whole.

The Arab League drew up a resolution following his suggestions which won unanimous support in the General Assembly. A few days later, a withdrawal of American troops from Lebanon was begun. By October the British troops were out of Jordan. The Arab nations came to an agreement of cooperation and mutual benefit which was spoken of as the Good Neighbor Policy.

"When it was all over, no one really knew which step had been taken before or after the other," someone said, and a UN correspondent wrote that the Secretary-General had solved the problem in a characteristic way.

" 'After the fireworks'; how much simpler life is, how much more difficult, how much *purer*, and how much more terrifying," Dag Hammarskjöld wrote at some time that year.

Other outbreaks of hostilities would follow. Agreements would be broken again and again. Conflicts would always arise over boundaries, political ideologies, and religious differences. The Suez Canal would be closed again to Israel's ships and to cargo bound to or from Israel. And there was still the unsolved problem of the Arab refugees—the first among problems, Hammarskjöld called it, saying that it continued to be urgent. But for the time being, another crisis which might easily have led to a world war had been averted.

Later, at a press conference the Secretary-General was asked if he felt that the United Nations would have greater influence and impact on the world if there were

stronger emphasis on moral condemnation of wrong-
doers. Hammarskjöld had no patience with people or
nations that assumed the right to pass moral judgment on
others. His answer was a curt "I am perhaps not a
moralist."

Another correspondent took up the same question. "If
UN decisions do not register moral judgments, what
should be the purpose of UN decisions?"

"They register judgments, and I hope they are
moral."

He had once written in his journal, perhaps after some
other remark of this kind: "Jesus' lack of moral principles. He sat at meat with the publicans and sinners, he
consorted with harlots. Did he do this to obtain their
votes? Or did he think that he could convert them by
such 'appeasement'? Or was his humanity rich and deep
enough to make contact with them, with that in human
nature which is common to all men, indestructible, and
upon which the future has to be built?"

He still wrote of his loneliness, not as often as before
he had taken on the duties of Secretary-General, but as
poignantly. He saw the contentment of his friends and
his brothers in their family life, and he followed the
growth of their children from babyhood through school
days. He was a favorite with them because he treated
them as people and did not try to talk down to them. He
explained in detail the art of skiing to the children of
Heinz Wieschhoff, his advisor on African affairs, and he
was as considerate and tender with the three children of

his Swedish aide, Count Wachtmeister. His brothers'
children were grown now, with families of their own,
and his friends, Bo and Greta Beskow, had their first
child, a little girl they named Maria.

"Why have you never married?" Dag Hammarskjöld was asked. He answered that in his childhood he
had seen the loneliness of his mother during his father's
long absences on public business and he would not want
to subject a wife to the same thing. On his 53rd birthday, in July, 1958, when he was in the midst of
negotiations with the Arab States, he had written:
"Did'st Thou give me this inescapable loneliness so that
it would be easier for me to give Thee all?"

In his role as international public servant working for
peace in every part of the world, he had little time for
visits to his native country. The farmhouse at Skåne was
too long empty. To escape for short periods to the
solitude he needed, he bought a house in the rolling hill
country around Brewster, New York. He wanted to
become as familiar with the surroundings of his new
home as he was of the mountains and moors of Sweden.
Books on the plants and wildlife of the region were added
to his library. Often, on a long hike up the wooded
foothills, he stopped to identify some wildflower that
grew only in this part of America or to watch a cardinal
and listen to its song of spring. He wrote an article, "The
Camera Has Taught Me to See," about photography, his
favorite hobby next to hiking and mountain climbing.

"When I look back at the results of my interest in
photography, which has always been intense," he

wrote, "the important thing is not the pictures I have been able to take, but far more the way doing this has taught me how to 'see.' It is better to teach oneself to see than to have one's vision fixed by others." He explained that this meant observing the play of line, the division of light, the balance of detail and totality. As an example, he described some of the pictures he had taken, which he especially liked: "An evening motif with a thunderstorm over the Chartres plainland, showing the play of forces around the Cathedral which, despite its hugeness by human measure, disappears as a futile detail in the shadow of the cloud; a Burmese woman sitting in devotion in front of a reclining Buddha; a bare oak branch where the lines reflect the balance between force and nervous sensitivity that Nature's own creations can so often display."

He was able to catch such images with words as well. In seventeen-syllable haiku poems, in which so much can be said with so few words, he points to a picture and lets the reader find his own interpretation.

A warm autumn night. A moon
Lighting this path—
Far away a heart stops.

April snow.
The cardinal sought shelter
In the white forsythia.

Trees quiver in the wind,
Sailing on a sea of mist
Out of earshot.

In the spring of 1959, Dag Hammarskjöld flew to Southeast Asia where, he said, he felt trouble brewing in the air. Diplomatic relations had been broken between Cambodia and Thailand. Laos and Vietnam, like Germany and Korea, were tragically divided into two governments, Communist and anti-Communist, which resulted in the inevitable bickering and hatred. Fighting had broken out in Laos, with aid for one side coming from the United States and, for the other, from the Soviet Union and Communist China. To prevent the country from becoming a battleground of the Cold War, he had talks with the king and with leaders on both sides. He was criticized because of his neutral stand, as he had been before and would be again, but his interest was in the country itself, coming out of colonialism and groping its way toward national unity.

Khrushchev, who had objected to the way he had handled the Suez and the Lebanon crises, invited him to Russia that summer. There he was treated with the diplomatic courtesy given a chief of state. Receptions were given for him; he met with leaders of Russia's collective farmers and visited the industrial fair; and one afternoon he was taken rowing on the Black Sea with Khrushchev at the oars. But this congenial mood did not last long.

In November Hammarskjöld accepted an invitation to return to Laos. There had been complaints that the Communists from North Vietnam were infiltrating into that country. There was a request for a UN Emergency Force like those used in Suez and Lebanon, but Hammarskjöld, after talking again with the leaders, decided to leave a personal representative to see that the country kept a neutral policy, to work out some internal reconciliation, and to give whatever economic aid was needed. He chose Edouard Zellweger, a Swiss diplomat and lawyer, who was an expert in the problems of underdeveloped countries. Instead of receiving aid from countries on either side of the Cold War, Laos would be helped by the United Nations through a technical assistance mission in agriculture, education, health, transport, communications, and public administration. This was met with objections from both the West and the Soviet bloc. A definite turn in Khrushchev's attitude toward the Secretary-General dated from that time.

At a press conference Hammarskjöld said that one of the things to be done with Laos was to imbue the country, torn as it was between East and West pressures, with a sense of direction. A few months later, in early 1960, a reporter asked again about Laos, which way the compass pointed—east or west?

Hammarskjöld's answer was one word: "Forward."

In March, 1960, the King and Queen of Nepal, who were in New York for a visit, invited Hammarskjöld to come to their country for discussions about boundary lines. It was a busy year for the Secretary-General, with new African nations receiving their freedom from colonialism and asking for admission to the United Nations, but he found time that summer to make the trip. This Himalayan kingdom, nestled as it was beneath the world's highest and most challenging mountains, held a fascination for him.

At a reception in his honor at Katmandu, the Nepalese capital, a government official asked him if he would like to fly to the eastern mountain ranges early the next morning before the hour of the official discussions. If so, the king would put at his disposal his personal plane and pilot. Mount Everest—Annapurna—Gauri Sankar! Dag Hammarskjöld was delighted with a chance to see them and made a secret wish that the weather would be clear the next day. But what a pity, he thought, to approach these mountains by plane and not by foot.

That night, after the reception, he went out for a late stroll with his aides and Bill Ranallo, his bodyguard. A Nepalese, who acted as their guide, led them through the narrow, twisting streets of the old city. The little cubbyhole shops were closed, the street vendors had departed for home with their unsold wares, and there was quiet after the clatter and noise of the day. A full moon shone and in its shimmering light the fantastic many-colored carvings on the temples and ancient palaces seemed to come alive.

The Nepalese asked Hammarskjöld if he would like to visit Swayambhunath, a great Buddhist shrine on a small hill rising up from the flat valley west of the city. Though the hour was late, he accepted. With all the meetings and discussions scheduled for his stay here, there would be no other time to see this famous shrine close to the birthplace of Buddha where men have worshiped for more than two thousand years. Besides, he wanted also to catch a glimpse from the hilltop of the Himalayas in the moonlight.

They drove as far as the car would take them; then

they got out and climbed, as so many generations of pilgrims have done, along the steep winding path that led to the top. There stood the main shrine, a dome of white stucco-covered brick with a gilded spire rising into the heavens. Hammarskjöld, in writing about it, described it as "dreaming its dream of a world beyond pain and vicissitude in the shadow of the timeless mountains."

The clouds drifted away, but an evening mist rose from the valley like a deep blue curtain drawn over the horizon. Although the mountains were hidden from him, he could feel their presence. It was small wonder the people living below held them sacred as the dwelling place of their gods. At the feeling of spring in the night air, Hammarskjöld's thoughts went back to Easter at Vezelay, half a world away, with its processions of pilgrims over the years.

A horde of monkeys came leaping down from the trees and approached them, breaking the stillness with their sharp chattering. Shrewd beady eyes searched for the offerings of rice or sweetcakes pilgrims always left in the small alcove shrines around the base of the large one. Between each of these shrines there was a tier of prayer wheels. Two Tibetan monks in high boots were walking around the large shrine, turning the prayer wheels as they passed, each turn sending up a thousand prayers to the gods.

One of the monks opened the doors to a side chapel which held a large statue of the Buddha. Silently the monk motioned to Hammarskjöld and his companions to enter. He then gave them candles and flowers for their offering. "To share with him his reverence for the mystery of life was easy in this setting, so intensely reflecting the endlessness of man's search and the greatness of the world to which he belongs," Hammarskjöld wrote. It seemed to him a fitting prelude to the morning's flight. Mountains so long revered should be approached in the spirit this visit to the shrine inspired.

The mist had disappeared with the rising sun the next morning, and the mountains beyond the bright green hills and valleys could be seen, surrounded by clouds and in all their rugged beauty. The king's plane was a DC-3, nonpressurized and without oxygen, which meant it could fly no higher than twelve or fifteen thousand feet. Dag Hammarskjöld, with his camera ready, sat with the pilot in the cockpit. The pilot, a young Sikh from North India, shared his enthusiasm for mountains. With a sure eye he found his way from mountain to mountain, through valleys and over the passes.

Hammarskjöld looked down on the scene below, bold, forbidding, terrifyingly beautiful. To him it was a world far beyond human comprehension, and of the harsh purity of crystal, yet in such immense proportion that beside it, man became as a grain of sand.

They came first to the twin-peaked mountain of Gauri Sankar, named after the Hindu god of destruction and his wife. Its name was well chosen, for no one had yet succeeded in climbing to its summit. Hammarskjöld, with the instinct of a true mountain climber, found himself speculating on a possible route up the south and most inaccessible wall, but the plane flew too quickly past, and it was soon out of sight.

They approached Mount Everest. Snow rose like a plume of smoke from its highest peak, blown by a raging wind. It was impressive in its sharp outline, but Hammarskjöld felt somewhat disappointed. From all he had heard and read about it, he had expected to see it standing out, unique in its grandeur, the way of Mont Blanc in the Alps. Here he saw nothing that would distinguish it from any other mountain. He thought of Hillary, gaunt and tan, struggling up the icy slopes in 1953 with his Sherpa guide Tenzing, the first to reach the mountain's 29,000-foot summit. He thought of the many others who had tried and had turned back in defeat. There were some whose bones lay buried beneath many seasons of snow.

After a day of official meetings and talks, the Secretary-General and his aides were taken on another evening excursion about the ancient capital. They came to a place outside the city called Twenty-two Fountains, named after a mountain stream rushing down a stone ramp, with water bursting out of its many openings. Here was a meadow surrounded by tall trees, with a view across the valley of the Swayambhunath shrine silhouetted against the moonlit sky. A group of pilgrims on their way to the temple had stopped at a resting place to prepare their evening meal, dotting the meadow with the glow of their charcoal fires.

At the side of the ramp there was a small, square pond built of stone, with worn steps leading down into it.

Beneath the shallow water lay a statue of the sleeping Hindu god, Vishnu. With the eye of an artist, Hammarskjöld saw the contrast of the moonlight playing on the wet figure of the sleeping god and the red glow of the fires burning a short distance away. There was a silence which he said could be found only in the mountains, a silence which one could almost hear, so intense it was. The pilgrims went about their affairs without a sound, taking no notice of the visitors.

Before leaving Nepal, Hammarskjöld asked if, on his way to Delhi, the plane could take him by way of the mountains to the west. The morning was perfect for a flight. Climbing in a half circle over wild ranges, they suddenly came upon Annapurna, standing majestically beautiful in quiet contrast to the rugged glaciers and rocks on the slopes leading toward it. To him it was like a temple built for giant gods. The pilot, in spite of the numbers of times he had flown this way, shared his awe. As they flew past, it seemed to Hammarskjöld that the plane dipped slightly when rounding the mountain with a gesture like the affectionate stroke of a fingertip.

> The brilliant notes of the flute
> Are heard by the gods
> In the Cave of Birth.
>
> Himalayan ice cliffs
> Beyond the hills
> Of Vezelay at Easter.

Apes. The moon woke them—
Round the world's navel revolved
Prayer wheels of steps.

A place of rest. Charcoal fires.
Deep in the mirror
Vishnu is at peace.

EIGHT

1960

So little was known about Central Africa
only a century ago that a large part of
it was marked by blank spaces on the
map. The people living there, isolated
from the rest of the world, went on with
their way of life in scattered tribal
groups, very much as their ancestors
had lived thousands of years ago. Except
for occasional slave traders or ivory
buyers or an unusually adventurous
hunter, they knew nothing about the
world outside until around 1870. Men
began coming in then from lands they
had not known existed. They made
their way past the cataracts of the Congo
River and penetrated into the jungles,
making treaties and claiming this land
for their king or country. The land and
the people they divided among themselves, with boundaries of their own
creation drawn on a map.

Within less than a hundred years,
through periods of suffering bondage

and ruthless exploitation, the African people had made the tremendous stride forward to take their place with the free nations of the world. It was not easy. They had not been a part of the centuries of slow development. Without having known the loom, the plow, the sail, or, in some places, the wheel, they were thrust into a world-wide communication. The few who did manage to receive an education had done so at mission primary schools where they were taught to read and write in a language not their own, and learned about a culture that had been no part of their background.

A growing demand for freedom had begun in the countries to the north, those with links to Southwest Asia and to the countries bordering the Mediterranean where civilization had its beginning. The British Sudan became independent in 1956, and others were following. By 1959 the movement had spread so that France and Belgium, as well as Britain, began preparations to give up their colonies in Central Africa.

At the beginning of 1960, a round-table conference was held in Brussels between the Congolese leaders and the government officials of Belgium. Plans were proposed which would lead gradually to independence for the Belgian Congo, allowing time for the people to prepare for self-government. But the Congolese were impatient. "Independence now!" The cry went up and was echoed from village to village. Cameroon had just been given its independence from France, with Somalia soon to follow. The Belgian government gave in to the demand and set the date June 30 of that year for the Belgian Congo's independence.

Before his visit to Nepal and while the Belgian Conference was still going on, Dag Hammarskjöld, with his
aides who were specialists on African affairs, made a tour
of all the African capitals south of the Sahara. He met
and talked with the leaders and with the students of
newly established universities. Wherever he went, he
found that intense nationalism that is part of every
freedom movement. He called it a healthy awareness of
one's individuality. In his talks he went back to his
favorite theme of a harmonious balance between this
national pride and a sense of international responsibility,
of feeling a part of humanity as a whole. Perhaps
nothing could have pleased him more than a remark by a
university student in Uganda. He had mentioned to the
student that it must be exciting at this time to be training
for professional work in Africa.

"Sir, I regard myself first of all as a citizen of the
world," the student replied. "But, that being said, I am
rather proud to be an African."

In the various countries Hammarskjöld visited, he
found extremely able people, but unfortunately there
were too few of them. In the Belgian Congo, to name one,
there were only seventeen university graduates out of a
population of nearly fourteen million. Universities had
been recently established in some of the countries, including the Belgian Congo, but they were few. Quality
would have to make up for quantity, Hammarskjöld
said.

He saw the tremendous tasks these emerging nations
faced. They would need help on a larger scale than the
United Nations, with its small budget, was able to give.

There must be money to build hospitals, schools, and industry. Technical training for engineers, doctors, and administrators was needed. Help in education was needed, not only in schoolteaching and book learning but in civic education, to allow the people, as free citizens, to form their own political judgments. And above all, the people needed moral support. "In fact, I guess that is the most significant," Hammarskjöld said, "because people and money and education do not mean a thing unless they are given and provided in the right spirit, through sympathetic understanding."

The United Nations through its various agencies would do what it could, but that was only a fraction of what was needed. Aid would have to come from the Big Powers, with the danger always before them that the new countries in their inexperience would be caught in a tug-of-war between East and West ideologies.

At a press conference Hammarskjöld was asked if the ideological trends in Africa were basically their own or were they the same old clichés repeated again.

"I do not think the rights of man is a foreign ideology to any people," Hammarskjöld answered.

Western philosophers and thinkers might have expressed themselves more eloquently on the subject, he added, but that did not make the idea a Western idea imposed on anybody.

At another time he was asked about the widespread rumor in the United Nations that, with so many African countries being admitted, the Big Powers would be reluctant to bring important questions before the General

Assembly because they did not want African and other underdeveloped countries deciding on these questions.

"Will you comment on this and discuss with us the question of whether the usefulness of the UN is being increased or diminished by the admission of new countries?" the correspondent asked.

To Hammarskjöld there was something shocking in the belief that new states would take irresponsible stands. "I myself do not believe it for a moment," he declared. "On the contrary, I believe that new States are likely to approach problems with very great seriousness and with a very great sense of responsibility."

A summit meeting for the Big Four leaders was scheduled for May 16, in Paris, to discuss disarmament and control of nuclear tests. In return for Premier Khrushchev's visit to the United States, President Eisenhower was invited to go to Russia in June. There were fresh hopes for a thaw in the Cold War and agreements that would lead to world peace.

Suddenly these hopes were shattered by an announcement from Russia, just eleven days before the Conference in Paris was to take place. An American plane had been shot down over Russian territory. The American government first suggested that the plane, a U-2, had strayed across the border from Turkey while on a weather research. The next day Khrushchev came out with the news that the pilot of the U-2 had been captured alive, that he had been shot down 1200 miles within the Russian boundary, and that he had confessed that he was on a spy mission.

This had repercussions over the whole world and took on an importance far out of proportion in countries that were masters at spying.

The summit meeting, however, took place—under great tension—on the day it was scheduled. The Prime Minister of Great Britain, the Presidents of France and the United States, and the Premier of the Soviet Union sat facing each other for the purpose of a peaceful negotiation, but the meeting was anything but peaceful. Khrushchev made his speech, accusing Eisenhower of treachery and of carrying on a bandit policy, and he declared that the Soviet Union would take no part in the conference unless the United States President apologized for his past aggression and punished those who were responsible. This the President refused to do, and on the next day of the meeting, the Soviet Premier was not present. To further humiliate the United States before the world, Khrushchev withdrew his invitation to Eisenhower to visit his country. Other nations took up the insult. Student riots in Japan prevented the President's visiting that country as he had planned. Peace for the world seemed far away.

Dag Hammarskjöld, who had followed these events with concern, felt that the Summit failure pointed out the tasks the United Nations must face. The reasons why the efforts to negotiate failed would be studied and discussed for a long time, and that was necessary, he said, so that the conclusions could be a guide for the future.

"Men may be criticized, their actions may be criticized, their words may be criticized, the methods may be criticized, and abuses of those methods may be attacked. That is not the essential thing, and that does not lead us forward. The problems which would have been taken up in Paris remain with us and require as much of our honest efforts as ever. They deserve our earnest attention. And they require renewed initiatives toward a solution—initiatives that should be wiser for what has gone before, but not envenomed by the feelings to which recent events may have given rise."

The advantage of taking up such questions as disarmament and banning the nuclear bomb through the United Nations was that the negotiations could be done quietly —"non-publicized diplomacy," the Secretary-General called it—and they would be free from concern over prestige or national interests.

The new nations, having a voice for the first time in world affairs, were watching the actions of the older and more powerful nations.

"We are the new boys at school," said the delegate from Niger. "We are just watching to see how other people behave."

The time drew near for the two African States, Somalia and the Belgian Congo, to be given their freedom. For the past ten years the British and the Italians, under the UN, had been preparing Somalia for the responsibilities of self-government. Young men were chosen for their intelligence and ability in leadership to be trained and educated in governing. Belgium was trying the opposite approach for the Congo. Instead of educating only a few of the brightest to rule over the masses, they were starting from the bottom to build upwards. In addition to one of the best universities in Africa, there were technical schools, physical training schools, hospitals for medical training. The same opportunities were within reach for all, and anyone with outstanding talent could go as far as he was able. How well this method would have worked will never be known.

There had been danger signals during the five months since the round table conference at Brussels in January. The people were growing restless and impatient for their freedom. Old tribal rivalries, kept subdued by the Belgians, were rising to the surface. Elections were marked by violence. Patrice Lumumba, who had the largest following, was chosen in the elections as prime minister and Joseph Kasavubu as president. The two men were tribal as well as political rivals, and both had risen to power through disturbances and riots.

The Secretary-General had some misgivings about how smoothly the Congolese would be able to make the transition from dependency to self-government. He could not go there for the Independence Day ceremonies; he had to be in Geneva for the opening of the Economic and Social Council of the UN during the first week in July. He sent Ralph Bunche as his special representative, with instructions to be prepared to stay for an indefinite time. With Bunche went a group of expert advisors under the direction of the Bureau of Technical Assistance operations of the UN, to work with the Belgian technicians who had chosen to stay on in the Congo. Hammarskjöld planned to visit South Africa and

both the newly independent countries when the Geneva
meeting was over.

King Baudouin of Belgium traveled to Léopoldville to
preside over the ceremony of granting the Congolese
their independence. There was a brilliant display of
uniforms, medals, and ribbons of honor. Speeches were
made, a band played, and a troop of Congolese soldiers
marched in parade, guns shouldered and arms swinging.
In all the little mud hut villages throughout the Congo
and in the segregated shanty settlements of the cities,
people gathered wherever there was a radio and listened.
They were barefoot, dressed in cast-off European gar-
ments, faded and torn, or wrapped toga fashion in
lengths of Manchester cloth. Their faces were tattooed
with the mark of their tribe.

Free Congo! For weeks before the election the politicians had been telling them about the wonderful things
that would happen when they were free. Now the white
man was no longer their ruler and they stood as his
equal. Now they would be called "monsieur" instead of
"boy," and the pronoun *vous* would be respectfully used
when they were spoken to, instead of the humiliating *tu*,
toi used for children and inferiors. In the cities and towns
they had seen the white man's houses, large and handsome behind walled gardens. They had seen the shops
filled with things they'd never hoped to buy. "All this
will be yours when the Congo's free," the politicians had
told them.

In the evening, after the wild parrots had flown
screeching to their roosts and velvety darkness had come

almost as soon as the sun went down, they drank palm wine until they were drunk. And they danced all night to the rhythm of a drum. In Léopoldville, the new prime minister, the president, the thirty cabinet ministers, members of Parliament and governors of the six provinces were celebrating with champagne. All over the Congo, in the forests and by the rivers, in tribal villages and in cities, the cry went up: "We are the masters now!"

Five days passed and the people still waited for the change they had expected. They saw the new leaders of the government ride past in chauffeur-driven automobiles, and they saw them move into the handsome houses behind walled gardens. But the people in the segregated settlements still wore cast-off clothes, slept on mats spread on a dirt floor, and ate pounded manioc and bananas fried in palm oil. And the soldiers still had to obey their Belgian officers.

On the fifth of July, the Congolese soldiers in two garrisons turned against their officers, beat them, and stripped them of all their clothes. After a short lull the rebellion flared again. Like a raging fire it spread from garrison to garrison, and now the civilian population joined in. They went on a rampage against the white residents who still remained—looting, robbing, raping, killing—with a savagery unknown in modern history.

Over three-fourths of the Europeans who survived fled in panic across the borders into Rhodesia, Ruanda, and Brazzaville. Belgium ordered six hundred paratroopers back to the Congo to protect its citizens' lives and prop-

erty. The Congo government protested, calling it an act
of aggression, but, with an army in revolt and completely undisciplined, the leaders were powerless.

A desperate Lumumba sent his Vice-Premier, Antoine
Gizenga, and several cabinet members to the American
ambassador in Léopoldville, asking for three thousand
American troops to get the Belgians out of the country.
They were told that aid would have to come through the
United Nations. They turned to the Soviet Union, and
then to Ghana, the newly independent African State,
and were given the same reply.

From the beginning of the trouble, Hammarskjöld was
aware of the need in the Congo Republic of far more
technical help than the UN was able to provide. Without
the help the European residents had been giving in technical service, medical care, and administration, the new
government faced a complete breakdown. There were
telephone calls and cables from Ralph Bunche to Andrew
Cordier in New York, and from Cordier to Hammarskjöld in Geneva, telling of the urgent need of help in
bringing the Congolese army under control. Hammarskjöld told Bunche to have the Congolese government
submit a formal request, asking for technical assistance
in the security field so that it could be brought before
the Security Council. He then postponed his African
visit and rushed back to New York to begin preparations.
A meeting of the Security Council was called for July
13.

On the day before, while waiting for the arrival of the
formal request, Hammarskjöld held a conference with

representatives of nine African States north of the Sahara. At this same time, twelve days after the Congo Republic's independence, Katanga, the richest of its six provinces in mineral resources, seceded and formed a separate state. Moise Tshombe, who was friendly to the West, complicated matters more by inviting the Belgians back to his province.

At the Security Council meeting the next night, the Secretary-General presented the request from the Congolese government. The problem before them was that Belgian troops were in the Congo without that country's permission. Whatever the reason, whether—as the Congo leaders charged—this was an act of aggression, or—as Belgium claimed—a humanitarian act to protect the lives of its citizens, it was a situation that could lead to serious international complications. He asked for a United Nations Force that would remain in the Congo until the leaders could take on the responsibility of restoring law and order. The Belgians then, he felt, would see their way clear to a voluntary withdrawal from all provinces, including Katanga.

A resolution was passed authorizing the Secretary-General to proceed in the way he had outlined. When the meeting adjourned in the early hours of the next morning, Hammarskjöld asked the Belgian representative to join him and his two aides on African affairs, Cordier and Wieschhoff, in his private office to discuss plans of withdrawal.

Word came from Léopoldville the next day that impatient Premier Lumumba had issued an ultimatum to

Ralph Bunche: if the UN Force did not have all the
Belgians cleared out of the Congo within seventy-two
hours, he would turn to the Soviet Union for aid.

The Secretary-General, realizing that the sensitive
new nation was too ready to suspect a return to subjuga-
tion, asked first for troops from the African States. Those
from outside must come from countries with no history
of colonialism.

Within forty-eight hours after the Security Council
voted on the military aid resolution, troops from Tunisia, wearing the blue helmets and arm bands of the
United Nations, landed in Léopoldville. Three days later
they were joined by men from Ethiopia, Ghana, Morocco, and Guinea. They were there, as in Suez and
Lebanon, solely in the interests of international peace,
with instructions not to fire a shot except in self-defense.
They were not to be used to promote one side or another
in internal conflicts.

The Katanga affair would have to be taken up later.
The army and police there were under control and
human life was not in danger, as in the rest of the country. The first thing of importance was to restore order in
the other five provinces where there was no order, and to
supply food and medical care where it was most needed.

By July 20, just a week after the first discussion of
the affair in the Security Council, Hammarskjöld was
able to inform the Council that the United Nations had
embarked on its single biggest effort under UN colors,
organized and directed by the UN itself. The Belgians
had begun to withdraw peacefully. "But," he added,

"we have in no way passed the corner." The next week he joined the troops in Léopoldville. To the British ambassador, he said, "This is the most difficult mission I have ever had to face."

Perhaps never before in history has a new nation come into existence under so much turmoil and confusion. Its people had missed the slow, painful climb by their own effort from tribe to community, and from community to nation. Free now of foreign rule, they brought the tribal law of the jungle to their new government, but without the strict tribal discipline their ancestors had known.

It was less important to Lumumba to bring order out of chaos than to get the hated foreigners out of the country and to have the Katanga province back in his power. He wrote a formal letter of complaint to the president of the Security Council, pointing out the slowness of the UN Forces in entering Katanga. Backed openly now by Russia, he demanded military assistance to crush Tshombe. Ralph Bunche was sent to Katanga to prepare for a peaceful entry of the Force, but he was told by Tshombe that, when the troops arrived, they would be met with all the resistance that could be brought to bear.

The Secretary-General decided to call off the operation for the time being rather than risk an armed conflict. He had pledged that there would be no shooting except in self-defense. He returned to New York to take the matter up before the Security Council. The Soviet Union and Poland accused him of giving in to the colonialists and

ABOVE, The United Kingdom's Prime Minister Harold Macmillan addresses a meeting of the General Assembly in September of 1960. Behind him are Secretary-General Dag Hammarskjöld, Assembly President Frederick H. Boland, and Andrew W. Cordier, Executive Assistant to the Secretary-General. BELOW, Dag Hammarskjöld inspects a Guard of Honor at Njili Airport shortly after his arrival in Léopoldville September 13, 1961. The Secretary-General made the trip in response to an invitation by Premier Cyrille Adoula (wearing dark glasses) to discuss United Nations aid and support to the Republic of the Congo.

The memorial cairn erected on the site at Ndola, Belgian Congo,
where the plane carrying the Secretary-General and members of
his staff crashed September 18, 1961.

demanded the troops be sent to shoot their way into Katanga. Guinea and Ghana, under Communist influence, threatened to withdraw their men from the Force and settle the Katanga problem themselves.

"I do not believe," Hammarskjöld said, "that we help the Congolese people by actions in which Africans kill Africans or Congolese kill Congolese, and that will remain my guiding principle for the future."

The problem could be solved only by a good diplomatic preparation, he felt, and he was backed in this by a resolution passed by the Security Council. Again he conferred with the Belgians about a peaceful withdrawal from Katanga, with the United Nations taking over their work in technical aid and advice in administration. He decided to add the well-disciplined Swedish troops to the Force. On August 9, he notified Moise Tshombe that he would arrive in Katanga the next day at the head of two companies of Swedish troops. He assured Tshombe, as he had done before, that the troops would be used only in connection with the Belgian withdrawal. When that was accomplished, the question between the central government in Léopoldville and the Katanga government would have to be taken up as a domestic matter, one in which the United Nations had no right to intervene. Tshombe replied that the Secretary-General would be received with courtesy. Hammarskjöld also notified Lumumba of his intentions.

"I will soon enter Katanga with all the members of my government," Lumumba declared. "My concern is to see that peace and order are restored immediately throughout the entire country. I am awaiting the Secretary-General to determine with him all the measures to be taken to implement the decisions of the Security Council."

The Secretary-General had no intention of allowing United Nations troops to be used to further political ambitions on either side. He notified the prime minister that the Security Council was concerned solely with the matter of outside intervention, as was true in the case of Lebanon. He also obeyed the demands of protocol by consulting with Gizenga, who was then in New York as the Congo government's representative at the UN.

When he arrived at Léopoldville, the Secretary-General stayed only long enough to gather together his Swedish troops and his military and civilian aides. Without seeing or notifying Lumumba or any other member of the central government, he went on to the Katangan capital, Elizabethville. There he talked with the Belgian commander and quietly worked out with him a schedule for the withdrawal of the Belgian troops. Within a week the withdrawal began, and the United Nations Force took over the key positions throughout the province.

On his return to Léopoldville, Hammarskjöld sent word through the Congolese Foreign Minister that he would like to report the success of his mission to the prime minister. Lumumba was in a rage. He refused to see the Secretary-General. He wrote letter after letter, each more violent in abuse than the last. Like a child in a temper tantrum, he listed his grievances and made demands.

"You are acting as if my government, which is the repository of legal authority and is alone qualified to deal with the United Nations, did not exist," he wrote. He considered it improper that the Secretary-General had conferred with Tshombe. Furthermore, African instead of Swedish troops should have been sent. The Security Council resolution of July 14 was to provide him with military assistance to subdue Katanga, he declared. He demanded aircraft placed at his disposal immediately, African troops flown in, the disarming of Katanga, and the Swedish troops withdrawn.

In his messages of reply Hammarskjöld explained, in as simple terms as he could, that the United Nations Force was committed to a policy of noninterference in domestic affairs. He waited two days while Lumumba fumed and raged and dictated more letters.

During this time, Hammarskjöld had a chance to see something of the work the United Nations Technical Assistance workers were doing. The plans were beginning to take shape, but they faced a tremendous task. There was food and medicine to be distributed, but doctors and nurses needed to be brought in to keep diseases and epidemics under control. Schools would have to be reopened and plantations made to produce again. Some of the engineers, who had escaped across the border, returned now that the United Nations troops were there to protect them, and transportation was being restored, with the opening of railroads and clearing of the river channels. There had been no one to man the towers at the airports or to operate the system of radio communications and beacons to aid air navigation. The technicians were now working toward getting at least the major airports back in service soon. The telephone exchange for local and international communications had to be operated and kept in repair, and farm machinery that was beginning to rust in the tropical climate had to be put back in order. Funds from the United Nations would also have to relieve the critical foreign exchange of the country.

At ten o'clock on his second night in Léopoldville, still with no agreement from Lumumba to a meeting, Dag Hammarskjöld returned to New York in the chartered plane that had brought him to Africa. The frustrated Lumumba, who had made the Secretary-General and the UN Force his sworn enemies, now turned to the Soviet Union for aid. Russian planes were ready and waiting to come in. There were seventeen, complete with crew, ten to be used for military purposes. Several hundred Soviet technicians arrived with one hundred trucks. They gave their aid directly to the government as the Belgians were doing in Katanga, instead of working through the United Nations as the other countries did.

Patrice Lumumba was a victim of circumstances. He came into power as head of a nation, lacking the maturity for the heavy responsibilities he must face. Whatever had been his aims in the beginning, he found himself courted by the big powers on both sides; he had been made to feel an importance out of proportion to reality. It was enough to turn his head. "I am the Congo!" he declared.

He was to have ten brief weeks of glory before his

government broke up into rival groups based on tribal hostility and ambition for power. Another province seceded, followed by more riots and massacres. President Kasavubu announced over the radio that Prime Minister Lumumba was dismissed. The next day Lumumba announced that President Kasavubu was dismissed. The quarrel and confusion among the Congolese leaders were echoed in the halls of the United Nations. Lumumba and Kasavubu each sent his own representatives to New York with demands to be recognized as head of the government. Lumumba, through his representative, added to his demands twenty aircraft, a large amount of guns and ammunition, and a powerful transistor radio. Kasavubu wanted UN protection of airfields and radio stations. The Council was divided in its support.

The Secretary-General could see the danger of the country becoming what Spain had been twenty-five years before, a battleground, he said, with fighting going on all over the prostrate body of the Congo and pursued for confused and conflicting aims. He asked the Council's support to help bring about a peaceful solution to the Congo's problems without outside interference by having all aid channeled through the United Nations. The Soviets bitterly opposed the resolution but, at an emergency meeting of the General Assembly, it was passed.

The opening of the Fifteenth General Assembly was scheduled for September 20, four days after the emergency meeting. More than a month earlier, Premier Khrushchev had announced that he would attend as Russia's representative. That spring he had disrupted the Disarmament Conference in Paris and it was obvious he was coming to the United Nations Assembly meeting for the same reason. He had persuaded the heads of all the Soviet bloc countries to attend, also those of the neutral countries he considered friendly. England, France, and Belgium sent their prime ministers. Never in history had so many heads of states been gathered in one place. President Eisenhower spoke at the opening meeting, then left.

The first business before the Assembly was admitting the new nations. One by one the names were called—the Republic of Cameroon, the Togo Republic, Somali . . . Thirteen African States and Cyprus became members of the United Nations that morning, bringing the number of African States to twenty-three. When the ceremony was over, the delegates of all but the Congo Republic took the places reserved for them, quietly and with dignity. Soon they were to witness the most turbulent session in the history of the United Nations, with Khrushchev shouting interruptions at other speakers or noisily shaking his fist in disapproval of what was said.

The following day he made his first speech before the Assembly. He started out with attacks on the countries he called imperialist, and he brought up again the matter of the U-2 plane captured over Russia. After two hours of this, he came to the real target of his abuse—Dag Hammarskjöld. He raised his voice in a shout and flung his arms, accusing the Secretary-General of misusing the UN Force in the Congo to serve the interests of the imperialists. His abuse went beyond that which had caused Trygvie Lie's resignation. He wanted to abolish the post of Secretary-General entirely and replace it with a group of three: one to represent the Western Powers, one the Socialists, and one the nations that remained neutral.

Dag Hammarskjöld sat beside the newly installed president of the Assembly at the high marble desk on the raised platform. Representatives from ninety-nine countries were in the audience that day. Looking out at the faces turned toward him, he must have wondered if there was a friend among them. To be strictly impartial, as he had been, is to be accused of partiality by both sides. In his effort to prevent war, he had been criticized for the way he had handled each crisis—Suez, Lebanon, Laos, the Congo, Katanga.

Khrushchev's speech came to an end at long last. There was wild applause from the Soviet representatives and their sympathizers, with the neutrals joining them somewhat doubtfully. As Khrushchev left the rostrum, he turned back with a grin toward the Secretary-General; he met no response.

The dignity of Hammarskjöld's reply was in sharp contrast to Khrushchev's speech. It was a question not of a man, but of an institution, he said. In exercising his right of reply, it was not to correct any factual mistakes or misrepresentations. That was unnecessary in the light of the very full debates in the Security Council and the Emergency Session. His reason for taking the floor was to make clear what was and was not the problem before the Assembly. It was no longer one of certain actions, but of the principles guiding them. He repeated the policy of neutrality as it had been stated in the Charter, and emphasized the need to be true to the letter and spirit of the Charter, whatever disappointment it might cause those who thought that they could add to their political weight by drawing the United Nations over to their side.

The Secretary-General spoke quietly, seemingly unaware of the thousand tense listeners taking in every word. *If* the office of the Secretary-General became a stumbling block because he stood by the basic principle which must guide his whole activity, *if* he came under criticism, such criticism struck at the very office and the concepts on which it was based.

"I would rather see that office break on strict adherence to the principle of independence, impartiality, and objectivity than drift on a basis of compromise," he said.

During the enthusiastic applause that followed the end of the Secretary-General's speech, Khrushchev began pounding noisily on the desk with his fist. A look of astonishment came from the Soviet delegates; then they, too, pounded at their desks, like schoolboys playing follow the leader.

A week later, on October 3, Khrushchev spoke again. He repeated his accusations that the Secretary-General had always upheld the interests of the monopoly-capitalist countries and had been prejudiced in his attitude toward the Socialist countries. "There is an old saying that there are not and never were any saints on earth. Let those who believe in saints hold their opinion: we do not credit such tales," he shouted.

Again the eyes of the listeners were turned toward the Secretary-General, but they could read nothing in his expression. He toyed with a pencil, sometimes made notes on a pad before him, but no sign of emotion crossed his face.

"To avoid misinterpretation," Khrushchev went on, "I want to reaffirm that we do not trust Mr. Hammarskjöld and cannot trust him. If he does not muster up enough courage to resign, so to say, in a chivalrous manner, then we shall draw the necessary conclusions from the situation obtaining."

Hammarskjöld had his reply ready, but he was advised by the Assembly president to wait until the afternoon, leaving everyone in the Assembly Hall wondering if this last insult would drive him to resign as Lie had done. During the lunch hour, he was joined in his private office by his aides on African affairs, Cordier, Bunche, and Wieschhoff.

The great hall was filled for the afternoon session. At three o'clock Dag Hammarskjöld came down to the rostrum. Again, his quiet speech was a contrast to the blustering accusations of the morning. It was a speech based upon calm reasoning. He repeated the words of accusation against him. Those who invoked history would certainly be heard by history, he said. He had no reason to defend himself or his colleagues. All before him were the judges. No single party could claim that authority. "Let the countries who have liberated themselves in the last fifteen years speak for themselves."

Again he said that it was the institution that counted and not the man. The man holding the responsibility of chief executive should leave if he weakened an organization. He should stay if his doing so was necessary for its maintenance. The Soviet Union's indication that it was impossible to work with the present Secretary-General seemed to provide a strong reason why he should resign. But he saw in the proposal of three executives to fill the post a weakening of the United Nations. By resigning, he said, he would at this difficult and dangerous time be throwing the organization to the winds.

"It is not the Soviet Union or, indeed, any other Big Powers who need the United Nations for their protection; it is all the others. In this sense, the organization is *their* organization, and I deeply believe in the wisdom with which they will use it and guide it. I shall remain in my post during the term of my office as a servant of the organization in the interests of all those other nations as long as *they* wish me to." Hammarskjöld's voice was low but firm.

"In this context the representative of the Soviet Union spoke of courage. It is very easy to resign; it is not so easy to stay on. It is very easy to bow to the wish of a Big Power. It is another matter to resist. As is well known to all members of this Assembly, I have done so before on many occasions and in many directions. If it is the wish of those nations who see in the organization their best protection in the present world, I shall now do so again."

There had been interruptions of applause during the whole of the short speech. Now, with these last sentences, a thunderous applause broke out. The delegate from

Tunisia rose to his feet. The United States delegate followed. One after another, the members of the whole
Assembly, except the Soviet bloc and a few of the neutrals, rose to give the Secretary-General a standing ova-
tion. Khrushchev sat at his desk, pounding the top with
his fist. At one point he took off his shoe and pounded
with that. He had been triumphant in breaking up the
Summit Meeting in Paris a few months earlier, but now,
in this quiet-spoken, well-mannered Swede, he had more
than met his match.

"The shoe-thumping fellow continues as a dark thun-
derhead to threaten all unrepentant non-Communists
with hail and thunder and probably locusts and other
plagues traditionally favored by tribal gods," Hammarskjöld wrote in a letter to his brother.

On United Nations Day, October 24, the scene in the
General Assembly Hall was in quiet contrast to the one
three weeks earlier. The portable stage had been put up
for a concert by the Philadelphia Symphony Orchestra.
It had been the custom to include the last movement of
Beethoven's *Ninth Symphony* for this yearly event,
but Hammarskjöld asked now for the performance of the
entire symphony. He made a short talk to the audience
in which he called the *Ninth* an enormous confession of
faith in the victorious human spirit and in human
brotherhood, a confession valid for all times, with a depth
and wealth of expression never surpassed.

"When the *Ninth Symphony* opens we enter a drama
full of harsh conflict and dark threats. But the composer
leads us on, and in the beginning of the last movement

we hear again the various themes repeated—a moment of silence and a new theme is introduced, the theme of reconciliation and the joy of reconciliation. A human voice is raised in rejection of all that has preceded and we enter the dreamt kingdom of peace." In this road from conflict to reconciliation, he continued, the composer had given them a faith and a credo which they might make their own. "We take part in the continuous fight between conflicting interests and ideologies which so far has marked the history of mankind, but may we never lose our faith that the first movement will be followed by the fourth movement."

The drama of harsh conflict and dark threats still hung heavily over the Congo, and the fourth movement of that "dreamt kingdom of peace" was far in the future. Patrice Lumumba was under a warrant of arrest, charged by Kasavubu with a number of crimes against person and state. To avoid arrest he retired to his home, a mansion on the banks of the Congo River, once the residence of the Belgian Governor-General. He appealed to the United Nations for protection, and a guard of Ghanian troops of the Force was stationed at his gates. Congolese troops were stationed a short distance beyond to see that he did not escape. Though he was surrounded by guards, Lumumba managed to keep in touch with the ministers still loyal to him. His Vice-Premier Gizenga had escaped to Stanleyville, his and Lumumba's own province, and was setting up a separate government there, accompanied by the violence, riots, and murder that had taken place in Léopoldville earlier.

Nine days after Lumumba's dismissal in the fall of 1960 and the breaking up of Parliament, Colonel Joseph Mobutu, the twenty-nine-year-old chief of staff, announced that, since the government leaders were fighting for power, the army would take over. Kasavubu remained president, but Mobutu brought in a group of young followers and put them in high positions.

Andrew Cordier had temporarily replaced Ralph Bunche as representative of the Secretary-General in the Congo. A short time later, Rajeshwar Dayal from neutral India was appointed to the post. Another neutral, Hammarskjöld's fellow countryman Sture Linner, was in Léopoldville as director of the UN Technical Assistance Organization.

On November 8, Kasavubu came to New York to appear before the General Assembly. After a bitter debate which lasted two days, his delegates were seated as representatives of the Congo Republic. A few weeks after this, on November 27, Patrice Lumumba escaped from his house in a black sedan, unseen by the UN guards or the Congolese soldiers. He was captured December 2 on his way to Stanleyville where he had planned to join Gizenga and was brought back to Léopoldville, bound and badly beaten. The next day he was taken to a garrison a few miles south of the capital.

Hammarskjöld sent messages to Kasavubu, reminding him of his obligations on human rights under the United Nations Charter. He demanded a fair trial with a public hearing and the prisoner's own choice of counsel. Kasavubu was bewildered. Why should the United Nations

be concerned over the fate of one who had turned so
viciously against the organization? he wanted to know.
He listed some of the former prime minister's crimes
which, he pointed out, the Secretary-General had himself deplored. Lumumba even complained because there
had been UN troops guarding him and keeping him from
the prosecution lawfully initiated against him. Hammarskjöld sent another message, requesting that a committee of the International Red Cross be allowed to visit
the prisoner and examine the place and condition of his
confinement. Kasavubu coolly warned against outside
interference in domestic affairs. He promised nothing
more than that he would abide by the provisions of the
Charter and that the prisoner would be tried by the rules
in force in civilized countries. Before the end of the year,
however, he gave in enough to allow the International
Red Cross to send investigators to visit Lumumba.

The departure of the Russian Premier had not ended
the attacks on the Secretary-General. They became
worse than ever after the arrest of Lumumba. The Soviet
Union charged the United Nations and Hammarskjöld,
whom they still called a lackey of the colonialists, with
being accomplices in this venture. Peking and the Com-
munist-front organizations of Asia and Africa echoed the
charges, and five neutral countries—Ceylon, Guinea,
Morocco, Indonesia, and Yugoslavia—threatened to
withdraw their troops from the UN Force in the Congo.

"We have been accused of servility in relation to the
West," the Secretary-General said in a statement before
the Security Council, "of softness in relation to the East,

of supporting this or that man in the Congo whom one
group or another on the world scene has chosen to make
its symbol, or for assisting another man to whom another group has chosen to tie their hopes for the success
of interests they wish to safeguard. However, this is no
excessive price to be paid for avoiding the thing for
which no one in my position should be forgiven: to
compromise, in any political interest, with the aims and
principles of this organization. It has not been done and it
will not be done with my knowledge or acquiescence."

A few days earlier, the day after Lumumba's arrest
when the new attacks began, Hammarskjöld had written
in his journal:

> The road,
> You shall follow it.
>
> The fun,
> You shall forget it.
>
> The cup,
> You shall empty it.
>
> The pain,
> You shall conceal it.
>
> The truth,
> You shall be told it.
>
> The end,
> You shall endure it.

He kept, on his bedside table, a French translation of
Thomas à Kempis' *Imitation of Christ*. Often, after a

weary day, he read before going to sleep such lines as: "Why seekest thou rest since thou art born to labor? Put thee to patience more than to consolations, and to bear the cross more than to gladness"; or, "My son, suffer me to do with thee what I will; I know what is expedient to thee."

Thoughts of sacrifice and death seem to have haunted Dag Hammarskjöld more than ever that year. Late in November he wrote a poem on the musings of Christ in the garden of Gethsemane, waiting, praying: "Nevertheless, not as I will . . ." The disciples slept and could not hear his call. Soon the torches, the kiss of betrayal, soon the dawn and the Judgment Hall. "What will their love help there? There, the question is only if I love them."

In a poem written December 2, the day of Lumumba's arrest, he might have had in mind the troops in Africa under the United Nations flag, surrounded by danger, and with orders to fire only in self-defense. "They paid the full price of love that others might enjoy a victory."

The turbulent Fifteenth General Assembly adjourned for the midwinter holidays on a world that would seem beyond all hope of peace. On Christmas Eve, Dag Hammarskjöld thought of the two Christian holidays symbolizing the Crucifixion and the Birth. How proper it was, he wrote, that Christmas should follow Advent—the Manger on Golgotha, the Cross in Bethlehem. He remembered one of the old Wallin hymns his father had loved:

'Strive, the pains of death endure,
Peace eternal to secure :
For the faithful and the tried
Heaven's Gates shall open wide.'
(*Archbishop J. O. Wallin, 1819*)

He turned again to the Psalms for comfort; and, as during the Suez crisis, he wrote :

" 'I will lay me down in peace, and take my rest; for it is thou, Lord, only that makest me to dwell in safety.' " (*Psalm* 4 :9)

" 'Thou hast showed thy people heavy things: thou hast given us a drink of deadly wine. Thou hast given a token for such as fear thee: that they may triumph because of the truth.' " (*Psalm* 60 :3–4)

NINE

1961

Soon comes the night! Another year was reaching its end. New York night clubs were crowded and the streets were filled with people in a mood of gaiety, taking little heed of the sharp winter wind. The clock at Times Square pointed to midnight and the chattering noise of passersby rose to a shout. Sirens shrieked, whistles blew, and horns honked from the passing automobiles. Strangers exchanged friendly smiles and acquaintances greeted each other under showers of confetti. The old year had passed and the new year, 1961, had just begun. "Happy New Year!" could be heard from one end of the city to the other.

On the 38th floor of the UN glass-and-steel skyscraper, high above the city's sounds, lights were still burning. It was Saturday, and the rest of the building was practically deserted except for an occasional night watchman.

Dag Hammarskjöld had spent the entire day in his wood-paneled office suite. One by one his aides had gone to their homes or to parties to celebrate the coming year. Only his executive assistant, Andrew Cordier, remained with him. They had little time to meditate on what 1961 would bring. The old year, in its last hours, had heaped problems enough upon them.

The representative from Laos had brought news of intervention again by Communist China and North Vietnam in that small and troubled country. Cuba claimed that the United States was secretly plotting an armed invasion. The Soviet delegate, carrying out Khrushchev's policy of boycotting the Secretary-General, had kept the information from him while he himself made preparations to call a meeting of the Security Council for New Year's Day. And as usual, there was trouble in the Congo. Colonel Mobutu's men were on a fighting expedition against a pro-Lumumba garrison at Kivu, a province in the eastern part of the country. They had gone there by way of Belgian-administered territory.

There was a busy hum of signals in the cable room on the 38th floor, with messages to and from the United Nations Technical Advisor in Laos, the Secretary-General's Special Representative in the Congo, and the Belgian authorities of the African Trust Territory Ruanda-Urundi. As for the Cuban situation . . . the Soviet aide to the Secretary-General was sent for and brought from a New Year's Eve party to Hammarskjöld's private office, where he was given a severe reminder of the United Nations Charter, and of the obligations of an international public servant. A new meeting of the Security Council was arranged for the middle of the coming week—through the office of the Secretary-General.

At one-thirty in the morning of New Year's Day, the Secretary-General and his aide at last closed the doors of their offices and made their way home, through streets now deserted by all but a few late revelers.

The representatives of the International Red Cross, who had been allowed to visit Lumumba in his prison on Christmas Day, reported they had found conditions there satisfactory. But on January 18, a few weeks after they had departed, mutiny broke out in the garrison where Lumumba was being held. Kasavubu, believing the mutiny was caused by soldiers who had come under the prisoner's influence and also seeing he had more than he bargained for in a prisoner whose treatment was being watched by the whole world, had Lumumba and two of his former ministers transferred to Katanga where they were turned over to Tshombe, his bitterest enemy. Those who saw them taken from the plane when it landed at Elizabethville reported that all three showed signs of having been badly beaten.

As soon as he received the news, Hammarskjöld sent a message to Tshombe, telling of the concern of the whole world in the fate of the Congo's former Prime Minister and his two companions. He pointed out, as he had to Kasavubu, that Mr. Lumumba was entitled to a fair trial under commonly accepted principles of law and human rights. "I am sure that pending a decision in this matter, you will see to it that they receive the humane and fair treatment to which they are entitled," he added.

Four days after they were taken to Katanga, Lumumba and his two companions were murdered, but the news was not given out by the Katangese government until they could keep it a secret no longer. Tshombe waited two weeks—Lumumba had been dead for ten days—before answering the Secretary-General's cabled message. He showed amazement, as Kasavubu had, that the United Nations should be concerned over a man whose guilt had been recognized by that organization.

The International Red Cross again sent their investigators. A United Nations Commission arrived, insisting upon seeing the prisoners. They were all turned away. Tshombe made excuses for the fact that no one was allowed to see Lumumba and his men. There were rumors and denials; then there came a report that the prisoners had escaped. Hammarskjöld sent another message to Tshombe, reminding him of the fugitives' right to humane treatment.

On February 13, a report was given out that Lumumba and his companions had been captured by a group of villagers and killed. The village was not named. Nor was there ever any trace of the victims' bodies.

The news was received with shock and horror throughout the civilized world. In many countries Patrice Lumumba became a martyr. Rioting broke out as if at a given signal. Belgian embassies were raided and stoned or burned. A few American embassies were also under attack.

Again Dag Hammarskjöld became a target for both sides. Many of the African and Asian nations carried out their threat, made at the time of Lumumba's arrest, and withdrew their troops from the Congo. In the Security Council, the Soviet delegate lashed out at the Secretary-General, repeating his charge of his being an imperialist lackey, and adding to that an accusation of his being an accomplice and organizer of murder. The neutral states sympathetic to Communism joined the Soviets in their demand that Lumumba's follower, Gizenga at Stanleyville, be recognized as the head of the Congolese central government. On the other hand, some of the Western powers accused Rajeshwar Dayal, the Secretary-General's representative in the Congo, of having closed his eyes to the outrages committed by Lumumba's men, while taking every opportunity to denounce the anti-Lumumba regimes. There were demands, to which Kasavubu added his voice, for Hammarskjöld to replace him. The Secretary-General was criticized in the West's press for the United Nations policy. It was called uncertain, its order fuzzy and limited.

" 'I became also a reproach unto them: they that looked upon me shaked their heads.

Help me, O Lord my God: O save me according to Thy mercy.' (*Psalm* 109 :24–25) "

It was Ash Wednesday, two days after the news of Lumumba's death had been received, when Dag Hammarskjöld wrote in his journal this quotation from the Psalms. He had addressed the Security Council that

day, defending his policy of neutrality, as he had had
to do so often. The United Nations had worked, through
efforts beyond the imagination of those who founded the
organization, to prevent the young African countries
from becoming a battleground for foreign powers as
Spain and Korea had been.

To be a roadblock to such efforts is to make yourself
the target of attacks from all who find their plans
thwarted, he said. "Member nations have not yet accepted the limits put on their national ambitions by the
very existence of the United Nations and the member-
ships of that organization."

A shipment of Soviet arms was already on its way to
Gizenga at Stanleyville, and the United States threatened
to step in if Russia intervened.

Again it was wondered if Hammarskjöld would offer
to resign in the face of the new and more brutal attacks.
He only repeated the statement he had made after Khrushchev's demand in October, 1960. By resigning at such
a time as this, he would be throwing the Organization to
the winds.

"It is ironic," he said, "for us who have been guided
solely by the interests of the Congo, to be attacked by
those who pursue entirely different aims."

A commission was set up to investigate the cause of
Lumumba's death and the disposal of his body, but the
Congolese leaders refused them entry into the country
and gave them no cooperation. To be morally judged
before the world for their actions in government was
something they had not expected, and it caught them

unprepared. They made statements and later denied them; they promised, wavered, and broke the promises. After all, they declared, it had been an internal matter in the first place.

There was more danger now than ever before of civil war and anarchy in the Congo, with one government at Léopoldville, one at Elizabethville, and one at Stanleyville. The Congolese soldiers were still resentful and perpetually on the verge of mutiny because conditions were the same for them under black leaders as they had been under white, and they were not given the luxuries the politicians had promised them. Half the army was under Mobutu and half under Gizenga. Katanga and Kasai, another province which had declared its independence, had their troops. Every tribal chief was ready to set up a government of his own.

"In the confusing fights and conflicts which have been going on for more than three months in the Congo among the political dignitaries of that country, an impression has grown that few have realized that to lead and govern is not a privilege to be sought for but a burden of responsibility to be assumed," Dag Hammarskjöld said.

In the past few years Hammarskjöld had been turning more than ever to poetry for relaxation from the cares of his office. In a poem he had started at the beginning of the Congo crisis and finished the following spring during the furor followng Lumumba's death, he wrote of a slave in ancient days led out to the arena.

He had watched others chosen for sacrifice. Now he

was the victim, strapped fast to the altar, his body "enduring the stoning, dumb when slit up and the live heart plucked out." He seemed to have seen in himself all who had gone through those last moments of waiting for the final sacrifice. One, lean and sunburned, walked between two wardens, tense but looking calm as he was led toward the wall, and to his execution. Another stood naked, nailed to the target by the first arrows. "And if their arrows hit, if their arrows kill, what is there in that to cry about? Others have gone before, others will follow."

On Whitsunday of that year, Dag Hammarskjöld seems to have found the answer to a spiritual search that had been carried on since his early youth:

"I don't know Who—or what—put the question, I don't know when it was put. I don't even remember answering. But at some moment I did answer *Yes* to Someone—or Something—and from that hour I was certain that existence is meaningful and that, therefore, my life, in self-surrender, had a goal.

"From that moment I have known what it means 'not to look back,' and 'to take no thought for the morrow.' "

On the wall of the 38th floor staff dining room, there hung an enlargement of the photograph he had taken of Annapurna, showing the contrast that had fascinated him between the majestic serenity of the summit and the wild and craggy ranges leading toward it. The Secretary-General used the photograph as an illustration of the progress made by the United Nations in the Congo. Step by step they were climbing, falling back at times, perhaps, but rising to push on toward the top. They were getting closer and closer.

New troops had replaced those that were withdrawn because of Lumumba's death. Nothing could turn Dag Hammarskjöld aside from his determination that the troops would be used only to keep the peace and not to interfere in putting one man in power or another one out. The staff of technical assistants was increased also. Food was distributed to the starving population. Over two hundred people were dying of starvation every day somewhere in the Congo. "I shall ask for more funds, much more," Hammarskjöld said. The need was very great.

In his speeches that summer and in his annual report for the General Assembly session, he stressed again the need for the highest standard of integrity in an international civil servant and an impartiality that rises above national loyalties.

After weeks of effort, with messages and cables going back and forth between the Secretary-General and the Congolese leaders, some kind of reconciliation had been brought about, with the promise of restoring a parliamentary government.

While the problems of the Congo seemed close to reaching a solution through peaceful means, there was a clash between Tunisia and the French stationed in Algiers. After an appeal to the Security Council from Tunisia, Hammarskjöld flew to the troubled area. Again, through what he called "quiet diplomacy"—private talks with the leaders on both sides of the conflict—the matter was settled and a serious crisis avoided.

In the middle of July, the new Congolese Parliament under heavy UN guard held its first session since the arrest of Lumumba and the military regime under Mobutu came into power. A new cabinet, representing all the Congo's six provinces, was approved unanimously by both houses. Neither Tshombe nor Gizenga attended, but they showed signs of cooperation and sent deputies to the meeting. Kasavubu remained president and, on August 2, he named Cyrille Adoula as prime minister, and the pro-Lumumba Gizenga became vice-premier for the second time. New ministers were chosen to represent all the political parties of the six provinces.

When the news reached the Secretary-General, he dictated a letter to Prime Minister Adoula, telling of his satisfaction with the new government: "As you are aware, the Security Council and the General Assembly have always attached the greatest importance to the convening of the Parliament and the establishment of a constitutional government. . . . I have no hesitation in confirming to you that the United Nations, in the activities with which the Secretary-General has been charged by the Security Council, will, in response to the decisions of Parliament, deal with your Government as being the Central Government of the Republic of the Congo."

That night, alone at his apartment, he wrote:

> Almighty . . .
> Forgive
> My doubt,
> My anger,

My pride.
By Thy mercy
Abase me,
By Thy strictness
Raise me up.

Again he went to the Psalms for expression of his thoughts and wrote: " 'Thou hast moved the land, and divided it; heal the sores thereof, for it shaketh.' (*Psalm* 60:2) "

There was reason for Dag Hammarskjöld to feel encouraged, but the long working hours and heavy responsibilities were taking their toll, and he began to show signs of fatigue that summer. "Tired," he wrote, "and lonely, So tired the heart aches." He pictured a mountainside, glacier-water trickling down the flat rocks. The climber's fingers are numb and his knees tremble.

Tired
And lonely,
So tired
The heart aches.
Melt water trickles
Down the rocks,
The fingers are numb,
The knees tremble.
It is now
Now, that you must not give in.

On the path of the others
Are resting places,
Places in the sun
Where they can meet.

But this
Is your path,
And it is now,
Now, that you must not fail.

Weep
If you can,
Weep,
But do not complain.
The way chose you—
And you must be thankful.

In early September he made a speech to his staff,
saying that those who had served the organization could
take pride in what had been accomplished.

"I know what I am talking about if I say, for example, that short of the heavy work in which each of
you has had his or her part, the Congo would by now
have been torn to pieces in a fight which, in all likelihood
would not have been limited to that territory, but spread
far around, involving directly or indirectly many or all
of the countries from which you come. I also know what
the activities of the Organization in the economic and
social fields have meant for a betterment of life of millions, and for the creation of a basis for a happier
future."

He spoke of their work and his as a contribution they
were permitted to make. "It is false pride to register and
to boast to the world about the importance of one's work,
but it is false humility, and finally just as destructive
not to recognize—and recognize with gratitude—that

one's work has a sense. Let us avoid the second fallacy as carefully as the first, and let us work in the conviction that our work has a meaning beyond the narrow individual one and has meant something for man."

On September 13, six days before the Sixteenth General Assembly was scheduled to open, Dag Hammarskjöld flew to Léopoldville, at the invitation of Premier Adoula, to discuss long-range plans for United Nations aid to the Congo. He planned, while in Africa, to pay a long-promised visit to Dr. Albert Schweitzer at his hospital in Lambaréné. From there he would go to Katanga, where United Nations troops were stationed, to see to the peaceful evacuation of Belgians and white mercenaries who had been drifting into the country.

Before leaving New York, Hammarskjöld took time to visit the Meditation Room. Always neat at his desk, he left his papers in order. Acting on the advice of his secretary, he mailed a letter to his friend Per Lind, who was now with the Swedish Foreign Office, asking him to take care of all his personal documents in case of his death. The manuscript of his journal was at his apartment in a desk drawer, with a letter to another of his friends in the Foreign Office, Leif Belfrage, giving him permission, if he thought they were worth publishing, to do so as "a sort of *white book*" concerning his negotiations with himself "and with God." The letter was undated and probably had been there through many a trip he had made to various parts of the world.

On the evening before his departure, he gave a dinner at his apartment for the director of the Stockholm National Gallery and the American artist Ben Shahn and their wives. The Swedish government wanted a portrait of Hammarskjöld to hang in the State Gallery along with the rest of the country's great national leaders. Shahn, who had been commissioned to do the work, planned to start the first sketches when Hammarskjöld returned for the opening of the General Assembly.

The men talked of their travels, and Hammarskjöld spoke of his visit to Nepal, a place which had, perhaps, impressed him more than any other. He showed his photographs of Mount Everest. The Congo was mentioned; he was optimistic about what was happening there. The worst was over, he said.

Andrew Cordier, who was with the group at the airport the next morning to see him off, expressed the same opinion.

"As far as Léopoldville is concerned, this will be the most pleasant of your trips there," he said.

"Yes, I hope so," Hammarskjöld answered.

Heinz Wieschhoff had been chosen to go with him because of his expert knowledge in African affairs, and as usual his bodyguard, Bill Ranallo, went along. Since the trip would be for less than a week and the General Assembly was not in session, Hammarskjöld did not appoint anyone to take his place as acting Secretary-General during his absence. Nor did he leave the methodical list of instructions he sometimes did on matters that might come up.

"If thou withdraw thyself from empty talk and idle wanderings, and from vanities and hearing of tidings, thou shalt find time sufficient and convenient to have sweet meditations," Thomas à Kempis had written.

His *Imitation of Christ* was the only book Dag Hammarskjöld had with him on the journey. Flying high over the Atlantic on the chartered jet plane with only his companions, there was time for meditation. News which they did not hear was then being flashed around the world: heavy fighting had broken out in Katanga between United Nations troops and Tshombe's men.

A man as sensitive as Dag Hammarskjöld could not have failed to sense the tension among those who met him at the Léopoldville airport. There were the usual newsmen and photographers who were on hand wherever he went. The Congolese dignitaries—Adoula, Kasavubu, Gizenga, and Mobutu—were there with ceremonial greetings. He inspected the honor guard of Congolese and United Nations troops and had a conference with the Premier at his residence to discuss the program for the two days he planned to be in Léopoldville. After that he was driven to the Léopoldville home of Sture Linner, the director of UN Technical Assistance for the Congo. It was not until then that Dag Hammarskjöld learned of what was happening in Katanga.

Often, when angry or annoyed, his face would flush. Now, it was noticed, the blood seemed drained from his body. His features remained impassive, but it was obvious the news had deeply disturbed him. The United Nations pledge to keep the Force out of national politics and to permit no shooting except in self-defense had been broken. The possibility of betrayal by someone in the

Organization, someone he had trusted, was the worst
blow he could have received. He asked pointed questions,
some of which were never to find satisfactory answers.
Who had given the order for the UN troops to open fire?
Why was it done just on the eve of his arrival in the
Congo?

He had a message sent immediately to his representative in Katanga to negotiate a cease-fire with Tshombe.
But Tshombe at that time was in hiding. The first message that had come from Katanga from the United Nations representative there was that the secession of Katanga was over. But the mercenaries began drifting back
to take up the fighting again, and Tshombe came out of
hiding. The reports now coming in were growing worse
and worse. The soldiers under the United Nations flag
were not equipped nor prepared for battle.

For four agonizing days Dag Hammarskjöld waited
in Léopoldville. Between the necessary state luncheons
and dinners with the heads of the central government,
he spent his time at the office assigned to him. There,
with his staff, he went over each message that came in
and drafted replies until three o'clock in the morning.

Fears were expressed by his New York staff that this
would mean a setback for the United Nations in the eyes
of the world. The member delegates were again divided.
The Soviets wanted an even tougher policy against Katanga. The United States was on the side of the Soviets
this time, with the Afro-Asian States agreeing. The other
Western Powers bitterly opposed the fighting.

The report came that a contingent of Irish troops had

surrendered, with fifty-seven claimed dead and ninety held as hostages. The Irish Premier sent word to the Secretary-General that the troops had been there to preserve peace and not to impose any particular solution in an internal affair. The Assistant Foreign Minister of Britain flew down to Léopoldville with a protest from his government.

Hammarskjöld admitted there had been serious military miscalculations, but he had no word of criticism or blame for the UN men in Katanga. He said that he fully accepted the responsibility for what had been done. However, he carefully checked each message that went out to the UN representative in Katanga, to make sure it was as he had dictated. In them he stressed the fact over and over that the United Nations troops were not to fire except in self-defense, and any new operations were to be cleared in advance with the UN representative in Léopoldville.

The Congolese Parliament met and passed a resolution to send troops to help the United Nations Force in Katanga, and Gizenga, as Lumumba had been before him, was prepared to head an invasion force. This, the Secretary-General refused, for it would mean the start of a civil war he was trying to avoid.

Every message that came over the radio must have seemed another arrow nailing him to the target. Reports of UN atrocities went out to the world from one side, and news of UN soldiers dead or wounded came from other sources. Some were troops that he himself had taken to Katanga with the understanding they would be there in the interests of peace only. A representative of the United Nations broadcast a statement from Elizabethville that his men would continue their operations in order to end the secession of Katanga. Hammarskjöld immediately sent a message to his chief representative, reprimanding him and the speaker for suggesting that UN troops were there to impose a political settlement.

The important thing now was to get in touch with Tshombe and to bring about a cease-fire agreement, and he urged this upon those in charge of the UN Mission in Katanga. The Secretary-General's face showed heavy lines of care. At some official function, an Indian bagpipe band played the Scottish funeral dirge, "Over the Sea to Skye," and he was seen to turn and stare at the players, but his expression showed nothing of his thoughts. At a dinner given for him by Kasavubu, he talked with an English newspaper correspondent with a frankness he seldom showed. He expressed his convictions on three issues. The continued presence of foreign elements in Katanga was a threat to peace not only of the Congo but of the world, he said. The United Nations must never become the hammer of the central government to bring Katanga to heel. And the aims of the organization, he continued, should be achieved without bloodshed.

At midnight on Saturday, three days after Hammarskjöld's arrival at Léopoldville, word came that Tshombe would meet the representatives of the United Nations Katanga Mission at Bancroft in Northern Rhodesia. Hammarskjöld came to the decision that he would meet the Katanga leader himself. He suggested that, since he would be going by air, it would be better to meet at Ndola, another border town in the British-owned territory, a few miles south of Bancroft.

Tshombe's reply was a conditional one. He requested that the UN troops be confined to their camps, that the UN stop troop movements and the sending of reinforcements by land and air. He requested also transportation by light plane capable of taking off from the airport at Kipushi. Another message was sent off from Hammarskjöld. There could be no question of anything but an unconditional cease-fire on both sides and an agreement to meet together. All other matters, obviously, would be discussed in the course of the meeting.

The message went off at noon on Sunday, September 17. There was no reply from Tshombe to the Secretary-General's last message. He and a group of his men were already on their way to Ndola. Dag Hammarskjöld, determined to put an end to the fighting as soon as possible and after that to try to bring about a reconciliation between Tshombe and Adoula, had decided to go on as he had planned, on the basis of his first message. All preparations for the flight had been made. A request sent to Britain for permission to hold the meeting in the British Colony had been granted. A protocol call was made on the Congolese Prime Minister to clear with him the proposed plans for the negotiations. He had chosen the members of the staff and the guards and security officers who would accompany him. There were ten, including himself, and six Swedish members of the crew. In his briefcase he had the papers and documents needed for the meeting, an extra shirt, and a toothbrush, and ten pages of the Swedish translation of Martin Buber's *I and Thou*, which he had been working on.

It was four o'clock in the afternoon before the Swedish Transair plane, the "Albertina," was ready to take off from the Léopoldville airport. The plane had been fired on and damaged while flying over Katanga the day before, but it had been repaired and was pronounced in good condition for flying. Bill Ranallo and one of the security officers, Sergeant Harold M. Julien had made a thorough search for possible sabotage.

Newsmen at the airport were told that the Secretary-General had nothing to say. They could only stand and observe as the passengers stepped on the plane. They saw Heinz Wieschhoff, Vladimir Fabry, an American special counsellor to Sture Linner, and Linner's Canadian secretary, Miss Alice Lalande, the only woman on board. Besides Ranallo and Julien, there were four men from the UN Force who went along as guards.

"Adjo," Dag Hammarskjöld said, in a Swedish good-bye to his friend Sture Linner who was there to see him off. Then he settled back in his seat in the cabin. He was always careless about fastening his seat belt, something which had caused Bill Ranallo many an anxious moment.

The reception committee, including the British High Commission in Northern Rhodesia, had been waiting at the Ndola airport from early afternoon until long after dark. Tshombe, who had arrived late, began complaining that he was tired and sleepy. At nine o'clock he was driven to the home of the Provincial Commissioner, thirty-one miles from Ndola. At last, at ten, the "Albertina" was seen coming in as if for a landing. The pilot radioed that he was descending and instructions went out from the radio tower. The plane circled west as if to make the turn to come down, then suddenly it disappeared into the darkness, with no more word.

The bewildered government officials waited, wondering the reason for this strange action. Except for a lower than normal altitude, the plane seemed to be in good position for a landing. Had the Secretary-General received an urgent radio message to turn back to Léopoldville? Had he changed his mind at the last moment about a meeting with Tshombe? No one knew quite what to do. They waited on until one in the morning; then they left to get some rest and sleep. The airfield had been deserted for five hours when, at dawn, the senior air traffic controller came on duty. He checked for news of the "Albertina," but there was none. It had not returned to Léopoldville. He then signaled the Northern Rhodesian capital and immediately messages went out to every landing place in that part of Africa, asking if there had been news of the plane. The Rhodesian Royal Air Force sent out planes on an organized search. From Léopoldville, the embassies of the United States, Britain, France, and Portugal, and the Congolese government responded at once to Sture Linner's plea for help by sending their Air Force planes. The United Nations in New York was notified and told to stand by.

The search went on all morning, with dozens of planes hovering over all of the Congo and the neighboring countries. It was one o'clock on that Monday afternoon of the 18th when the smoldering wreck of the "Albertina" was spotted in a jungle just nine miles away from the Ndola airport. Rescue workers had to make their way through dense undergrowth to reach them. Dag Hammarskjöld's body was found some distance away from the charred area, clutching in his hand some of the grass and leaves from the ground where he lay. Only one of the passengers, Sergeant Harold Julien who had also been thrown clear of the flaming wreckage, was still alive when he was found. He was never to regain consciousness enough to explain the mystery. The little information that he could give during his last hours was that Mr. Hammarskjöld said to turn back. There was an explosion. It was over the airfield.

Had there been sabotage or treachery? Or had the plane, damaged in flight the day before, developed trouble? And had Dag Hammarskjöld, seeing there would be a crash and explosion at the landing, given the order to turn away to save the lives of those waiting at the airfield? The answer will never be known.

Moise Tshombe, when told of the news, said, "This is a sad day for me. I knew him as a man I could talk freely with." Two days later he signed a cease-fire agreement, ending the eight-day battle with the United Nations Force.

The Sixteenth General Assembly opened as scheduled on September 19. All eyes were turned on the empty chair at the right of the Assembly president. Everyone stood, with heads bowed in silent prayer.

"He died, one might say, on the battlefield of peace,"

said the newly elected president, Tunisian delegate Monghi Slim.

All the flags of Sweden flew at half mast to mourn Dag Hammarskjöld and the two Swedish infantrymen and six Swedish members of the crew who died with him. Diplomats and statesmen from all over the world gathered at the Cathedral in Uppsala for the funeral services. Vice-President Lyndon B. Johnson and Adlai Stevenson were there to represent the United States. The King and Queen of Sweden sat at the right of the flag-draped coffin before the high altar. At the left were Bo and Sten Hammarskjöld with their families.

The Archbishop who had conducted the funeral services for Hjalmar Hammarskjöld seven years before chose the words of a Swedish hymn for the text of the service: "East, west, north and south, the arms of the Cross stretch bridging. All who dwell on earth and build, they are brothers."

An open gun carriage drawn by four horses, used only for royal funerals until now, bore the coffin from the Cathedral to the family grave in the quiet, tree-shaded cemetery. University students, wearing the traditional white cap and uniform Dag Hammarskjöld had once worn, lined the narrow streets, forming a guard for the procession. Walking silently behind the Hammarskjöld relatives to the mournful sound of tolling bells were people of every race and every faith, from nations large and small.

In the guest room of Sture Linner's home in Léopold-ville where Dag Hammarskjöld had spent his last night, there lay on the bedside table the book *Imitation of Christ*. A bookmark showed the page he had last read: "Even the blows and the punishments which we receive from that paternal hand would be gentle, since he would never allow misfortune to befall us except for our good."

On the bookmark were typed the words of the oath Dag Hammarskjöld had taken when he became Secretary-General of the United Nations.

"I, Dag Hammarskjöld, solemnly swear to exercise in all loyalty, discretion, and conscience the functions entrusted to me as Secretary-General of the United Nations, to discharge these functions, and regulate my conduct with the interests of the UN only in view, and not to seek or accept instructions in regard to the performance of my duties from any government or other authority external to the organization."

Bibliography

GAVSHON, ARTHUR L. *The Mysterious Death of Dag Hammarskjöld.* New York: Walker & Company, 1962.

GORDON, J. KING. *United Nations and the Congo:* A Quest for Peace. Carnegie Endowment for International Peace. New York: Taplinger Publishing Company, 1962.

HAMMARSKJÖLD, DAG. *Markings.* New York: Alfred A. Knopf, Inc., 1964.

HAMMARSKJÖLD, DAG. (Wilder Foote, editor) *Servant of Peace:* A Selection of the Speeches and Statements of Dag Hammarskjöld. New York: Harper & Row, 1963.

KELEN, EMERY. *Hammarskjöld:* The Dangerous Man. New York: G. P. Putnam's Sons, 1966.

LASH, JOSEPH P. *Dag Hammarskjöld. Custodian of the Brushfire Peace.* New York: Doubleday & Company, Inc., 1961.

LIE, TRYGVE HALVDAN. *In Cause of Peace:* Seven Years with the United Nations. New York: The Macmillan Company, 1954.

MEIGS, CORNELIA. *Great Design:* Men and Events in the United Nations from 1945–1963. Boston: Little Brown, 1964.

SÖDERBERG, STEN. *Hammarskjöld: A Pictorial Biography.* New York: The Viking Press, 1962.

STOLPE, SVEN. *Dag Hammarskjöld: A Spiritual Portrait.* New York: Charles Scribner's Sons, 1966.

Index

This book may be kept

FOURTEEN

A fine will be charged for each

MAR 18

APR 28